LEAD THE CHANGE

THE COMPETITIVE ADVANTAGE OF GENDER DIVERSITY AND INCLUSION

KELLY L. COOPER, M.A.

Advance Praise for *Lead the Change*

Inclusiveness is not only a social issue but also a key business driver. Diversity & Inclusion needs to be a strategic priority for any leader, and this book is a must-read for anyone wishing to leverage this competitive advantage.

*– **Virginie Hotte-Dupuis**, Chef communications externes & philanthropie, L'Oréal Canada*

I am really thrilled to support Cooper's book that inspires action from leaders and executives on Gender Diversity & Inclusion. Sodexo knows that gender balance fosters creativity and innovation and ultimately drives better business results. When women reach their full potential, business and society are stronger and more successful. I definitely think this book will be helpful to leaders and organizations.

*– **Normand St-Gelais,** Director of Corporate Responsibility, Sodexo*

Lead the Change is a terrific guide to creating gender inclusive, diverse, and equitable workplaces. It clearly outlines a pathway for the initiatives, competencies, and policies that are critical to move forward in a positive way. Having been personally involved in Kelly Cooper's innovative approach of tackling this issue on a sector-wide basis, I know this approach should be celebrated and emulated. Read and study this book as soon as you can!

*– **Michael Kaufman**, Author, "The Time Has Come. Why Men Must Join the Gender Equality Revolution" and member of the G7 Gender Equality Advisory Council, 2018 and 2019*

Cooper shows us that leadership matters and that we can all make a difference – no matter where our organization might be on the Diversity & Inclusion continuum. She combines the value proposition for GDI with a blueprint on how to effectively move an organization to be more diverse and inclusive. If you fear failure, have concern that your team won't buy in, or that your metrics won't tell you the story you want, this book will alleviate those concerns and motivate you to take action.

– **Derek Nighbor**, *President and Chief Executive Officer, Forest Products Association of Canada*

The financial and business case for Diversity & Inclusion is clear and well documented, yet achieving it remains an elusive goal for many companies and sectors. The insights and tools shared in Cooper's book can help companies better understand – and ultimately overcome – their barriers to lasting Diversity & Inclusion in the workplace, bridging the gap between ambition and achievement.

– **Felix Lee**, *President Prospectors and Developers Association of Canada*

Augmented by practical global leading-edge examples, any decision maker reading this book will have a logical and clear path toward shifting their organization toward a more inclusive workplace culture. A great read!

– **Tanya Wick,** *Vice President People & Services, Tolko Industries Ltd.*

Editorial Project Management: Front Rowe Seat Communications, karen@karenrowe.com

Cover Design: Shake Creative, ShakeTampa.com

Inside Layout: Ljiljana Pavkov

Printed in the United States of America

FIRST EDITION

Library of Congress

ISBN: 978-1-9992867-0-5 (paperback)

ISBN: 978-1-9992867-1-2 (digital)

To my late father and mother, Keith and Carol Ann, for instilling in me a strong sense of independence as well as the life experiences that built my confidence to speak up and have difficult conversations.

"Be the change you wish to see in the world."

Mahatma Gandhi

Table of Contents

LEAD THE CHANGE

THE COMPETITIVE ADVANTAGE OF GENDER DIVERSITY AND INCLUSION

A Note on Terminology

■ Gender Diversity and Inclusion

Broadly, diversity is any aspect that can be used to differentiate groups and people from one another. In practice, it means respect for and appreciation of differences in ethnicity, gender, age, national origin, disability, sexual orientation, education, and religion. But it is more than just a list. We all bring with us diverse perspectives, work experiences, lifestyles, and cultures. As a source and lever of innovation, diversity, and in particular "diversity of thinking," has a critical part to play. At the board level, it is a dimension that negates "group think."[1]

The Society from Human Resource Management (SHRM) defines inclusion separately from diversity as "the achievement of a work environment in which all individuals are treated fairly and respectfully, have equal access to opportunities and resources, and can contribute fully to the organization's success." (Note: Inclusion in Canada also refers to Indigenous peoples as recognized in Section 35 of the Constitution Act, 1982.)

■ Gender Equity vs. Gender Equality

The concepts of gender equity and gender equality are often confused. "Gender equality" means men and women having access **to the same opportunities**, regardless of their gender. "Gender equity" is a means to achieve gender equality. By putting in equity measures, you create equality. It means treating women and men **fairly**, which may or may not mean equal treatment.

I help organizations with gender **equity** measures (implementing the strategies and measures needed to compensate for women's historical and social disadvantages, which prevent women and men from otherwise operating on a level playing field) that will lead them to gender equality (equal enjoyment by women and men of socially valued goods, opportunities, resources, and rewards) in their organizations. Note that a gender-equitable approach is not about giving women jobs over men or relaxing standards for hiring women, but rather, it's designing policies and programs, including skills training, to support men and women so they may enjoy a more equal outcome.

Introduction:
A RETURN
ON SOCIAL
INVESTMENT

C an you remember the days when garbage was simply garbage? The days when, from diapers to cans and everything in between, we'd pitch it in the same bag and not even think twice?

Then came the 1990s, and our thinking about garbage changed forever. An environmental movement took hold and forced business leaders to think about treating garbage as a commodity. The C-suites of large corporations were asked to reconcile the environment and the economy—to find a financial return on the environmental good, while at the same time not wreaking havoc on the environment. As we all now know, the "3 Rs" are the best way to manage waste. We started to reduce, reuse, and recycle our garbage using recycling bins and composting, and there's been no looking back.

Fast-forward to today. Now we are seeing business leaders pressed to figure out how to make a *social* return on their investment. But just how this works is a new frontier still waiting to be fully realized.

It used to be that people thought a social investment meant a company sponsoring little Johnny's or Jenny's soccer team or giving funding to various stakeholder groups so they can participate in an environmental assessment process. Although such "investments" are well and good, they don't create a financial return to the bottom line. So, then what exactly *is* the right way to do this?

Sustainable development is a term that arrived on the world stage in 1992 with the Rio Declaration. This United Nations (UN) document was formed by all member countries and, for the first time, spoke about the need to take care of "the commons." The vision was to ensure that business was conducted in a manner that did not compromise the environment and/or social issues in favour of the economy.

The "commons" includes such things as our air, oceans, biodiversity, and a host of other important environmental issues that countries rely on from others to keep healthy. This UN document also spoke to the social issues that we all need to address no matter where we live, and one of those social issues was equal opportunity for women in society. This included the need for women to be able to work in a harassment-free place and to have a level playing field for job opportunities, including equal pay, among other aspects.

These are large topics that require incredible coordination across a country, let alone the planet, and therefore take considerable time to change. Having worked in the area of sustainable development my whole career, I'm quite familiar with the slow pace of change. My work has included studying the socio-economic aspects of landfill site selections in the greater Toronto area; representing Canada at United Nations meetings on sustainable development and climate change; and writing policy decision-making documents for Canadian federal government Ministers on nation-wide environmental assessment projects, the Oceans Act, Indigenous economic development, and more. It takes tireless effort to educate and inform people on the merits of pursuing these types of "greater good" issues. But I have also benefited from the reward of pursuing a better way—perhaps one can even say a more ethical way—of doing business.

In 2012, having toiled in the areas of environment and economy for twenty years in the private, not-for-profit, and public sector vantage points, I started thinking about changing gears and pursuing the social aspects of sustainable development. I had grown tired of the "old boys' network" that dominated those subject matters and was looking to make a difference on other issues. After some research and reflection, I realized that the social return on investment wasn't so much about external social investments, but internal ones. *Investing in the people* inside an organization by improving the quality of their work environment, optimizing their ability to innovate and perform, and reducing sick leave and turnover rates is not only good for employees but also improves the bottom line.

I have seen firsthand how a work environment that nurtures and values individual strengths, perspectives, and skills and creates a place of energy that inspires people to show up with their best leads to heightened loyalty to the organization. Plus, the reputation of the organization benefits as well. With this notion now front and centre in my mind, I set out to specifically seek improvements for women—to improve their opportunities and make things equal for them in the workplace.

The Equal Approach

I began going about my research, gathering data on women in the workplace, and speaking with women across many sectors about their experiences, and I started to figure out a path forward to affecting a culture change in the workplace.

As I have furthered my knowledge and understanding about this issue—spearheading national sector action plans on gender diversity and inclusion that had me working with private, public, not-for-profit, academic, and Indigenous senior representatives—it has become clear to me that we must change the paradigm on this conversation from a "women's issue" to an everybody issue.

Men and women alike, regardless of race, religion, or sexual orientation, need to be given a work environment that optimizes their performance and eliminates any source of harassment. This *equal* approach to the way the workplace operates will have a domino effect on our society—one that improves not only the workplace but also the home front.

My vision is that every woman, regardless of her race or religion, can truly feel supported by her partner, her workplace, and indeed by society to choose the life she wishes to have, free of harassment. It is a vision in which she can feel a sense of belonging to whatever sector she chooses to work in. And also, it's a vision in which a man will be able to leave work early on a given day to see his son's or daughter's activities without fear of missing out on upward advancement in the company—one in which men can be stay-at-home dads without the social stigma of being "that dad" who is perceived as a slacker.

A 2018 report issued by McKinsey Global Institute titled "Delivering through Diversity" makes a valuable assessment of how the social issue of diversity and inclusion is playing out in business today. Their conclusion was that this is no longer a matter of social justice or legal compliance, but that gender diversity and inclusion (GDI) represents a distinct advantage for modern-day organizations. In fact, a study done on over 1,000 companies in twelve countries found a clear correlation between "diversity in the leadership of large companies and financial outperformance."

McKinsey also found the following:

- Diversity and business performance are positively correlated.
- Leadership matters.
- Gender is only the tip of the iceberg, (i.e. inclusion is also important).
- The failure to change will cost you.

We'll touch on each of these factors throughout the following pages. For now, the bottom line is that gender diversity and inclusion are tied directly to your company's performance and growth.

It's not just a matter of social justice anymore. It's a matter of good business.

As a businesswoman in my company, the Centre for Social Intelligence, I coach leaders, conduct gender gap audits, develop gender strategies, and spearhead national sector action plans that focus on improving gender diversity and inclusion in organizations.

I believe wholeheartedly in the necessity and effectiveness of implementing gender diversity and inclusion in the workplace. I have seen the social and economic benefits of doing so through work with my clients and beyond.

While conducting research for this book, my conviction that this movement is the way forward for corporations and for our culture as a whole has only grown. But who am I, and why should you listen to me? How did I come to be doing this kind of work?

To be honest, diversity and inclusion wasn't always on my radar. I started my career in environmental science, and my work took me to the Arctic, Africa, India, and various natural resource sectors in Canada. Throughout the course of my experiences—some of which I'll share with you in this book—I came to understand that gender diversity and inclusion isn't purely a social justice issue. On a practical level, it's just plain good business. I've learned that how it is presented to decision-makers and how to harness this issue into a business line is key to its successful adoption. Eventually, this field became my specialty.

Whether my work has been about the oceans, Indigenous rights, climate change, large infrastructure projects, or gender equality, my career opportunities have allowed me to be on the cutting-edge of progress to our society. Over the last decade, I've taken on work experiences that have pushed the boundaries on how we can think about the environment and the economy, and I've turned my attention to the social issue of gender equality.

A social return on investment is definitely not clear to most people right now. That is what compelled me to write this book—to share my vision and knowledge to date on actions that can be taken right now to help leaders with this important evolution in workplace culture.

23

From the UN to the Corporate Boardroom

The Rio Declaration of 1992 spurred the creation of the UN Women organization, which has convened at an annual conference ever since, but it was in 1995 when all participating UN countries took the next major step and developed the "Beijing Declaration and Platform for Action." The Platform for Action clearly established a global strategy for promoting gender equality and highlighted the necessity to ensure that gender equality is a primary goal in all areas of social and economic development.

It was through the UN that the term "gender mainstreaming" was created and defined as:

> The process of assessing the implications for women and men of any planned action, including legislation, policies or programmes, in any area and at all levels. It is a strategy for making the concerns and experiences of women as well as of men an integral part of the design, implementation, monitoring and evaluation of policies and programmes in all political, economic and societal spheres, so that women and men benefit equally, and inequality is not perpetuated. The ultimate goal of mainstreaming is to achieve gender equality.[2]

Mainstreaming includes gender-specific activities and affirmative action whenever women or men are in a particularly disadvantageous position. Gender-specific interventions can target women exclusively, men and women together, or only men to enable them to participate in and benefit equally from development efforts. These are necessary, temporary measures designed to combat the direct and indirect consequences of past discrimination.

You can see that the initial intent of creating gender equality was always to include the involvement of men. But somewhere along the way, the limelight shifted away from this aspect and became focused solely on women. Of course, we need to raise awareness of women, but *including men in that conversation is key to making things equitable.* I am a firm believer that we must have both women and men working collaboratively to make a difference in diversity and inclusion.

It's hard to believe that the Platform for Action was introduced twenty-five years ago. We are now starting to see those high-level intentions move into corporate circles and boardroom tables. I am happy to be a part of making sense of this topic for many in the business community and to play a part in opening their minds to their corporate potential.

There is greater awareness now than ever before on gender imbalance in the workforce. Progressive leaders are looking to improve their reputations with all key stakeholders on gender diversity and inclusion and avoid being singled out for harassment issues. Society has elevated its social standard and is vocalizing the social imperative for gender equality across the work front and the home front. But what has been lacking is *how* to go about making that change happen.

I have experience working with leaders to implement gender diversity and inclusion (GDI) strategies. More specifically, I help companies achieve success financially while improving workplace culture overall. By understanding their goals and ambitions for the company—whether the organization is local, regional, or international—we work collaboratively with leaders to create a return on their social investment.

The purpose of this book is to engage leaders on compelling reasons why they should target gender equality as a business imperative and how to go about it efficiently. This book highlights several leading companies, such as Sodexo, that have invested in GDI strategies and have seen amazing results. For every dollar put toward gender diversity and inclusion, they have seen a return on investment of $19.[3] Readers will come away with a solid understanding of a path forward to shift the workplace culture toward this end.

This book is intended to help any senior leader in any sector understand the impetus behind the cutting-edge issue of gender diversity and inclusion, and how, by pursuing a culture shift in their organization, they will have a leg up on the competition in this ever-competing global market, both through financial returns and a more welcoming work environment for all.

Many of the concepts outlined in this book come from my experience and knowledge gained by developing a GDI strategy for sectors and companies. I wrote it for any decision-maker in any sector who is looking to learn the value proposition—how to *be* the change, *make* the change, and *leverage* the change... and translate it into dollars.

I hope that after reading this book, you'll see the incredible benefits—socially and economically—of leading the change toward a workplace culture that benefits women *and* men.

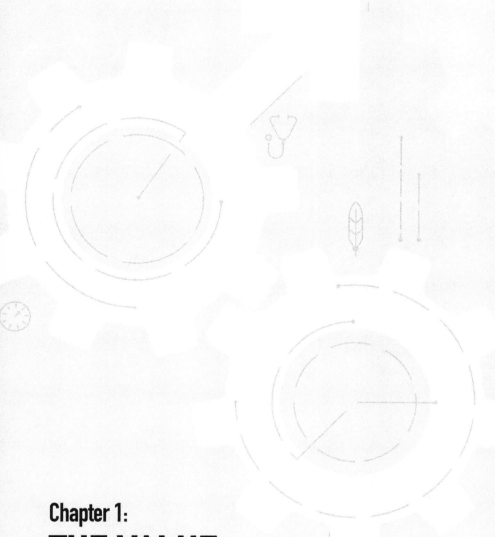

Chapter 1:
THE VALUE
PROPOSITION

I n keeping with the advice Wayne Gretzky's father gave him, decision-makers know that it's critical to anticipate where the puck is going in order to get into position and score.

Being able to see "the next big thing" is what can differentiate successful companies from the pack and propel them forward financially, while simultaneously motivating employees through a sense of pride in working there. Leadership comes from stepping up and out—often when others don't see the benefits yet—and bringing employees along to make fundamental change happen. And one of the issues that requires fundamental change is gender diversity and inclusion.

Although there are some who still have their heads in the sand, those of us above-ground are seeing the signs and messages all around, poking us and reminding us that change is coming regarding what our workforce needs to look like.

Legislation on gender diversity and inclusion is popping up around the world, and the number of female university graduates—including the science, technology, engineering, and mathematics (STEM) fields—is increasing. Women are chomping at the bit to get working and take on a career path to the boardroom or in technical positions. Shareholders are now asking questions regarding how many women sit on boards, and they are asking companies to be transparent with their numbers on gender diversity. Goldman Sachs just came out with a headline stating that "boards packed with bros don't get IPOs.[4]"[5] These types of messages send a pretty clear signal that an all-male board no longer cuts it, and if you want to get capital, you must diversify your gender composition. These are solid indicators that change is afoot.

In spite of these indicators, however, many decision-makers are still asking what exactly the value proposition is. What is the business case, or as I like to call it, the business *advantage*? Let me begin by answering this and lower the fog index so that we can get past questions about why we need to do this and get on with how to make it happen.

The Importance of Timely Course-Correction

Over the years, I have witnessed firsthand the importance of accurately predicting the course of the proverbial puck—seeing the change *before* it happens and adjusting accordingly. I have also learned that seeing what's coming isn't enough. It's the ability to convince others of imminent change that really moves the needle.

Back in 1992, when I graduated from the University of Toronto with an environmental science degree, the environment industry was hardly up and running yet. I went to the yellow pages and looked up the few meagre listings for environmental companies at that time, called each one of them on my landline, and asked if they were hiring. The effort paid off, and I was fortunate enough to land my first "real" job with an environmental consulting firm in Toronto. I was one of five environmental scientists hired to study the socio-economic impact of a landfill site selection project in the Greater Toronto Area.

There were five potential landfill sites, and one of them was assigned to me. My job was to cold call those who lived next to or near the potential landfill, ask to meet with them, and conduct an in-person interview about what the social and economic impact would be to them if the landfill were to go in their area.

Clearly, these were not going to be happy people.

I knew I had my work cut out for me, but I didn't hesitate to get on the phone and line up my interviews. I was always met at the door with anger and frustration about the issue at hand, but inevitably, after a two- or sometimes three-hour interview at their kitchen table, I would leave on good terms—sometimes with fresh-cut flowers and vegetables from their garden. One time, I was asked if I could come back and babysit their kids!

My boss was always amazed when I came back to the office with all these goodies. I guess that's why, at the end of that project, when they only wanted to keep one of the five of us on, I was asked to stay. Although flattered by the offer, I had other ideas about what I wanted to do and had another offer in the wings to work at the Ontario Environment Industry Association, an offer I ended up accepting.

When I look back at that experience, I see that it taught me so much beyond socio-economic issues surrounding a landfill. It taught me hands-on emotional intelligence skills like empathy, self-awareness, assertiveness, and flexibility, among others. I also learned the importance of engaging in difficult conversations, the importance of having others feel heard, and correcting misinformation when necessary.

What is the Business Advantage?

A pretty common question on the topic of gender diversity and inclusion is, "Why would we want to bother doing anything on this issue in the workplace when there is no clear imperative to do so? Things are fine as they are!"

Here is what I say to that. We don't have the luxury of debating this conversation anymore.

As I have shared, I started in the field of environmental science; I wasn't even dialled in to the issue of gender diversity and inclusion back when I was just beginning my career. It wasn't until later, when I started having kids, that it became quite evident to me that there was an issue. That's a time when women are either supported to advance and continue with their careers or pulled off the rails.

To be clear, gender diversity isn't just about supporting ambitious women. Rather, it goes beyond the personal career interests of individuals. We have to look more broadly and recognize that we *need* women for our economy to function at its best.

A Powerful Engine for Economic Growth

More women working means more money flowing into the economy and more taxes being paid, which translates to better infrastructure, more access to health care, and more desperately needed social services. That financial injection into the economy gives us a booster shot to compete in this global market. And the finances improve for a company due to many business factors.

Let's look at why I call it a business advantage for companies. These factors include simply increasing the number of women in the workforce and creating a powerful engine for economic growth; improved performance in the workforce, which translates to higher profits; improved innovative thinking and ability to be nimble in an ever-increasing, globally competitive market; and better business outcomes due to greater diversity of thought around options analysis of a particular problem or issue.

Consider these facts: A 2019 International Labour Organization survey of 13,000 companies found that, as a result of efforts to achieve gender diversity:

- 60 percent reported increased profits and productivity.
- 57 percent reported an increased ability to attract and retain talent.
- 54 percent reported greater creativity, innovation, and openness.
- 54 percent reported enhanced company reputation.
- 35 percent reported a better ability to gauge consumer interest and demand.[6]

In other words, gender diversity resulted in anywhere from 35 to 60 percent improvement in the company. Now, why would anyone say no to that? In fact, over 75 percent of CEOs already consider gender equality to be a top business priority, according to McKinsey's 2016 *Women Matter* report.

Company leaders aim to be responsible corporate citizens in the communities where their companies do business. They recognize that women make up half the population, so it's logical that they make up half the workforce.

But there is a disconnect. Despite the awareness of the moral, social, and economic advantages of a diverse workplace, less than 20 percent of decision-makers and corporate board members across all sectors are women. Certain sectors, such as computing, architecture, and engineering, fare even worse in terms of gender diversity, even though women are expanding their skills in STEM disciplines, which are in high demand by employers.[7]

McKinsey Global Institute found that, among 92 percent of the companies surveyed, women held less than 25 percent of the top jobs, even though 63 percent of those companies had at least twenty initiatives in place to address gender equity. That is bad news! Clearly, organizations are not going about this properly if those are the results.

▷ Climbing an Unstable Ladder

Years ago, before starting at my new job at the Ontario Environment Industry Association, I was asked through a peer at university if I'd like to go on a ten-person research expedition in the Arctic for two months to study the riparian zone of the Hood River in Canada. This was an incredible opportunity to go somewhere that most people only ever dream of going, and to be able to conduct research, too. There was no question I was going.

The PhD student who needed others to join him to collect data was from the University of Colorado, as were all the other students. I was quickly nicknamed "Token" because I was the token Canadian. We had a half-male and half-female crew. One twosome became romantically involved, but there were never any issues with harassment or troubles of any kind.

My arctic expedition was the most physically and mentally challenging trip I've ever experienced. We traversed 185 kilometres from the head of the Hood River to the Arctic Ocean using blow-up kayaks. We had food flown down the river every two weeks (which meant we had to get there in time to get more food), and there wasn't another soul to be seen outside of our group the entire time. There were, however, many caribou, arctic foxes, a muskox, and one incident with a bear. The sun didn't set for a large portion of our trip, and the water was so fresh that we could dip our cups in the river and drink straight from it. It was magic. I felt like I was on top of the world in more ways than one.

Once back from my arctic adventure, I began working immediately in the environment sector, doing consulting gigs so I could save up money to travel to Africa. I was passionate about being in the wild and loved observing wildlife and being around animals.

Earlier on in January of 1993, I had just turned twenty-two years old, and I headed off to Kenya by myself. I travelled on my own for about a week before meeting up with a group of other young travellers, and over the course of two months, we tented from Kenya to Zimbabwe. It was awesome. I was in my natural habitat.

I fell so in love with Africa that I wanted to get a job, stay, and live there. I read in the local Harare, Zimbabwe newspaper that they were looking for a park ranger. I thought, "I can do that!" so I decided to apply.

When I went into the government office and asked for an application, they took one look at me and laughed. I found out later that only men—and only local men, at that—would be considered for such a job.

Looking back now, I see how naive I was. But at the time, I felt deflated and sad that I wasn't even a contender because of my gender. It was one of the first times my gender played a direct role in taking an opportunity off the table.

The reality is women's prospects for promotion fall off at every step of the ladder. A McKinsey survey of 130 large companies revealed that while women made up 37 percent of the total workforce in 2012, they comprised only 22 percent of middle managers, 14 percent of senior managers and vice presidents, 9 percent of executive committee members, and 2 percent of CEOs.[8] Again, yikes!

▷ Market Stability and Economic Advantage

Ethnic and cultural diversity on executive teams is also remarkably low.[9] McKinsey conducted another study, based on U.S. and U.K. data sets. They started with university graduates to examine ethnically and culturally diverse representation among companies. They found that Black Americans comprise 10 percent of U.S. graduates but hold only 4 percent of senior executive positions. Latinos/Hispanics comprise 8 percent of graduates versus 4 percent of executives, and Asian Americans comprise 7 percent of graduates versus 5 percent of executives. As expected, white executives are represented to a greater extent on these teams, with nearly 85 percent of C-suite positions versus 68 percent of US graduates. Furthermore, they found that companies with the most ethnically and culturally diverse boards worldwide are 43 percent more likely to experience higher profits.

This discussion isn't just about the economic benefits of gender diversity in the workplace. The reason diverse work environments hold the key to market stability is that they are more inclusive, catalyze higher engagement, and enhance the entire organization from workers to customers to other stakeholders, as well as prospective employees.[10]

Women have a lot to bring to the table. In fact, in the U.S. they're better educated than men. According to the National Center for Education Statistics, women were to earn over 57 percent of all bachelor's degrees in the 2018–2019 school year, 58.4 percent of master's degrees, and 51.7 percent of doctorates.[11] This means that there is a growing talent pool of experienced and educated women ready to meet critical skills needs. In some countries such as Norway, legislation is even adapting to ensure that the economy is primed to take advantage of what women have to offer, including acts that prohibit discrimination based on gender, pregnancy, or work leave in connection with child care responsibilities. Additionally, a provision went into effect on January 1, 2020 to increase accountability through reporting duties.[12]

To summarize, we have companies aware that something ought to be done and that there are women of all races who are educated and interested in working in all fields. Plus, we have evidence that supports the fact that having women in senior roles is particularly impactful to the bottom line. We also need to factor in that the baby boomer generation is retiring, and we have a labour market shortage on our hands.

We live in an increasingly complex world that demands the brightest at the helm to combat whatever awaits and to help solve the world's most pressing issues. This is why I say we have no more wiggle room to mess about debating this issue. And it makes it all the more perplexing that people are dragging their feet.

Having more women in all parts of the economy and the workplace—from the boardroom to the C-suite to the mill floor—can be a powerful engine of economic growth in Canada and around the world. For example, increasing the number of women in the workforce has been one of the most powerful drivers of economic growth over the last 40 years, accounting for approximately one-third of per capita growth in Canada's real gross domestic product (GDP).

According to RBC Economics, if men and women participated equally in the workforce, Canada's GDP could be boosted by as much as 4 percent. A 2017 report by McKinsey Global Institute found that gender equality in Canada could add $150 billion to Canada's GDP by 2026—6 percent higher than business-as-usual scenarios. Even more compelling evidence points to opportunities for global economic growth. For example, in 2015 the Organization for Economic Cooperation and Development (OECD) estimated that a 50 percent reduction in the labour market participation gender gap across OECD countries would lead to a 6 percent increase in GDP. And in 2017, the World Economic Forum suggested that closing the global gender gap in labour market participation by 25 percent could add an additional US$5.3 trillion to GDP globally by 2025. This is a powerful incentive for companies and governments alike to accelerate efforts to achieve gender equality and inclusion across the entire economy.

Faced with the fact that if women were to play an identical role in labour markets to that of men, annual global GDP would increase by $28 trillion by 2025, there is little room to argue. Gender diversity isn't just a moral and social issue but a critical economic advantage.

The above statistics aren't shared to fill empty space here. They should be a serious wake-up call.

A comprehensive report by McKinsey Global Institute identified several types of interventions necessary to close gender gaps. (Note: I've paraphrased what this means for us in parentheses.)

1. Financial incentives and support (Meaning we need to incentivize people to choose diverse cultures through bonuses. For example, if a manager has a diverse team, he or she gets a 10 percent bonus.)

2. Technology and infrastructure (for example, baseline tracking of data)

3. Capability building, advocacy, and shaping attitudes (Think skills development and communications.)

4. Laws, policies, and regulations (for example, legislation on equal pay for equal work)

It may sound like a tall order for all of these components to shift, but the cost of *not* working toward these goals is so high that, when fully understood, there is no choice but to prioritize a shift toward gender-diverse work environments.

We will look more closely at these interventions later in the book. For now, just note that these are some of the key game-changer categories that, when executed on an enterprise-wide basis, get real results.

Enhanced Performance and Profitability

Evidence shows that enhanced performance of diverse work environments makes an even greater difference during an economic downturn and in the early stages of recovery. A 2012 study by Credit Suisse found that the financial benefits linked to having women on boards were more pronounced in the post-2008 period than in the three years leading up to the stock market crash. The researchers concluded that gender balance on the board brought greater stability throughout the market cycle.

I like this factoid. It puts to rest all the commentary I often hear from people who say, "We can't do it now, we are in a downturn, and we simply can't afford to do that!" But, as you see, by dealing with this workplace culture issue, you can improve the economics in ways not seen before.

Here are some more statistics to bolster the case on why gender diversity and inclusion equals good business sense:

- A 2014 Gallup study found that gender-diverse business units have 14 percent higher average revenue and 19 percent higher average quarterly net profit than less diverse units.
- A five-year study of company performance conducted by MSCI Inc. found that boards with at least three women directors are nearly 50 percent more profitable than those with none.[13]

- A 2015 report from accountancy firm Grant Thornton calculated the cost of just one year of poor gender diversity among executive board members in India, the U.S., and the U.K. to be *$655 billion*.[14]
- Research from the Peterson Institute for International Economics also shows that having more women leaders in business can significantly increase profitability. Their 2016 study of almost 22,000 firms across the globe has shown that a company with 30 percent women leaders can add up to 6 percentage points to its net margin, compared to other companies in the same industry.[15]
- PricewaterhouseCoopers (PwC) (2018) estimates that if Organization for Economic Co-operation and Development (OECD) member countries increased their female labour market participation rate to the same level as Sweden (80 percent), this would boost GDP by over US$6 trillion.[16]
- The World Economic Forum (2017) predicts that if the global gender gap in labour market participation is closed by just 25 percent by 2025, an additional US$5.3 trillion would be added to GDP globally.[17]

Further research supports gender diversity and inclusion as a business advantage. Studies suggest that having even 30 percent of a corporate board be composed of women directors can represent a critical mass in impacting company performance.[18] Companies with more women in leadership positions also outperform their competitors on a number of key financial measures, including share performance, stock price growth, return on sales, return on equity, and return on capital.[19]

A Catalyst study found that companies with the highest representation of women enjoy a 35 percent higher return on equity and a 34 percent higher total return to shareholders.[20] Other studies suggest that these increases can be as high as 53 percent on return on investment and 66 percent on return on invested capital.[21]

In addition, a 2016 report found that organizations with inclusive cultures are also twice as likely to meet or exceed their financial goals and eight times more likely to achieve better business outcomes.[22]

Still questioning if this is worth the effort? Okay. I have more to tell you.

Increased Innovation and Agile Decision-Making

Coming back to Toronto after my time in Africa was quite a culture shock. I didn't like the confines of the concrete jungle and was even more committed to ensuring that the environmental wonders of our world be kept intact. Very soon after my return, I was hired by a large environmental engineering firm to conduct environmental impact assessments.

At the time, I didn't know anything about gender inequality. It didn't even strike me as an issue. I was studying science, and I thought nothing of it. But, on reflection, there were not that many women studying science thirty years ago. At the engineering firm, I was one of only two women among sixty employees who weren't administrative staff. I grew up with three brothers in a patriarchal home, so being around guys and knowing (for the most part!) how they thought was completely familiar; a male-dominated work environment didn't faze me.

My job description was divided fifty-fifty between environmental assessments and business development—a result of my personality and my refusal to be intimidated by men. Seeking funding was something I thrived on. I loved the rush when you are successful with your idea, your pitch.

While within the office environment or out marketing the company, I was often subjected to men hitting on me. This was a different experience for me, in that guys usually treated me as one of them because of my ability to "talk their language." Yet I also had the features of a woman, so they felt that flirting was somewhat safe. I would dismiss them, and we would carry on, but some situations definitely got out of hand. From having a senior executive practically climb onto my lap in the back of a taxi to getting a steamy sex letter from a co-worker straight out of the blue, I swear to you nothing surprises me anymore.

Overall, greater diversity in the workplace means a broader range of leadership styles, experiences, and approaches to problem-solving and collaboration. It also provides an increased ability to gauge consumer interest and demand. Ultimately, this can result in enhanced team performance and greater innovation at all levels.[23]

▷ Growing a "Healthy Forest"

> I've been on many teams over the course of my career where I've been the only female, and I've been able to add ideas to the conversation that the men I was working with just didn't see. It's not like I'm Einstein, I just think differently. We all do. And so, the richness of diversity is that we can think things through thoroughly.

> We only gain by putting our ideas through this comprehensive lens. You may be discussing a spatial issue, like building a house and figuring out where a room would best fit. For the sake of the client, a female perspective can offer many insights. And so it is with many decisions that are made. The broader the reach is for input on a given project or problem, the higher the likelihood for innovative and effective solutions.

> I also reflect on my science background and think about how it applies to gender diversity and inclusion. How does it apply, you ask? Because in nature, we need diversity for things to thrive and have optimal performance.

Take a forest, for example. A forest made up of only one type of tree makes the forest susceptible to disease and pests. But if you have many different species in the same forest, the chance of the forest being decimated by disease or pests is greatly reduced. I believe the same is true in the workplace. A forest of men is susceptible to macho-man behaviours that, frankly, don't raise the bar on respect or innovative thinking in the workplace. The same goes for all women. Diversity of thought results in a strength of ideas that can keep your organization running at its best.

Research from Harvard Business Review has shown that diverse teams can develop more innovative ideas. When people from diverse backgrounds work together, their unique perspectives often lead to greater creativity. The study also found that diverse teams were more likely to have some common experiences with their customer or client base, which led to creating better products.

Diverse work environments aren't just attractive to employees. A diverse workforce signals competent management, which is attractive to investors. Gender diversity demonstrates to investors that a firm is well-run. For example, more diverse boards typically reflect a wider range of skills and experience, which can lead to greater accountability, enhanced governance practices, and improved collaboration. This, in turn, can help increase investor interest and confidence.[24] Sociological research on market valuation suggests that investors value when firms use commonly accepted best practices, such as the inclusion of diverse groups in hiring, and penalize those that don't. Research has even shown an increase in stock prices after firms win an award related to diversity initiatives.[25]

By most measures, the global business community is becoming more supportive of women and of women's importance in the economy. This shift has a domino effect, and firms that support gender diversity will capture these benefits earlier, leading them to step ahead of their competitors.

In addition, studies suggest that women in the workplace employ a broader range of leadership behaviours that improve organizational performance and are critical to a company's ability to tackle new kinds of challenges. For instance, women tend to employ more participative decision-making while also emphasizing the importance of developing people and serving as role models to others within their organizations.[26]

Interestingly, the only bank left standing after Iceland's 2008 banking collapse was women-run.[27] Productivity and innovation in a company can be enhanced by increasing the number of women employees and creating the work environments that will keep them in the company and leverage their contributions.

Leaders are recognizing that innovation is driven by diverse talent and that they must attract and retain the best and brightest people in order to remain globally competitive. Experts around the world are warning of talent shortages in many parts of the global economy. Canadian women are among the most highly educated in the world.[28] They are uniquely positioned to help address this talent shortage.

I've given you a lot of facts and figures to digest on this issue, but I still have more.

Better Business Outcomes

Business outcomes are defined here as improvements to employee health and safety and less risk-taking behaviour, leading to overall improvements in the workplace.

Studies validate the link between a gender-diverse workforce and improved health and safety performance.[29] Adding women to a group of men, either in a crew setting or at a board meeting, can provide insights on options that consider greater safety.

▷ Employee Safety

More than 97 percent of all reported workplace fatalities in Canada between 1993 and 1995 were men. Workplace injuries are also predominantly male and can result in significant costs: $9.7 billion in Canada for the direct costs (including workers' compensation, health care, and rehabilitation) associated with occupational injuries in 2008 alone.[30] In part, this reflects the preponderance of men in higher-risk industries; however, it also reflects gender expectations and attitudes that can influence men's willingness to engage in risky activities, as well as their reluctance to seek help.[31]

Gender-diverse boards tend to be more active in overseeing strategic direction and practicing objective decision-making, and studies continue to prove that companies with gender-diverse boards consistently outperform those with all-male boards. One of the contributing factors here is that having more women in the workplace can cultivate a culture of care and a safety-orientation that offers new options for women *and* men. This, in turn, can make critical contributions to not only employee wellbeing but also overall corporate performance.[32]

As outlined in a report I contributed to for Women in Mining Canada, there are distinct commonalities between workplaces that encourage greater participation by women and those that maximize employee satisfaction and engagement. In both cases, costs related to illness, injury, and turnover are reduced, all of which strongly impact an organization's bottom line. In addition, these organizations experience reduced employee stress, increased teamwork, and lower absenteeism.[33]

Case studies have linked gender-diverse organizations with the cultivation of company-wide devotion to safety. By contrast, workers in typically male-dominated (and traditionally dangerous) workplaces, such as coal mining operations and offshore oil drilling platforms, tend to feel pressured to appear infallible. It's not difficult to see how a culture that values a machismo-based self-image would lead to workers pushing themselves too hard, which naturally contributes to unsafe behaviours.

Gender-inclusive workplaces, meanwhile, tend to seek safer and more ergonomically efficient ways to move heavy items. But women aren't the only ones to benefit from such measures. Men too reap the benefits of less wear and tear on their bodies from repeated physical strain.

Less employee turnover has the added benefit of fewer inexperienced workers, which reduces the risk of lost-time, accidents and injuries. In fact, according to Women Building Futures, an organization devoted to training women for careers in the construction trades, women graduates are more open to coaching and treat equipment well, leading to fewer incidents and reduced repair costs.

▷ Employee Retention

Another business outcome that stems from greater involvement of women, particularly in senior roles, is a decrease in the turnover of staff.

The cost of implementing a GDI strategy is far less than the cost of losing staff and going through the arduous process of seeking, finding, training, and building relationships with new staff members. This is an example of the costs of not having gender-diverse teams. Decision-makers aren't aware of these costs—and that doesn't even include the cost-benefit analysis in the literature regarding gender diversity and inclusion.

Turnover is reduced when teams are gender diverse—and this works both ways. Female-dominated teams can benefit from the addition of males too. Anytime only one gender is around the table, there are costs associated with a lack of productivity and innovation.

Workforce capabilities and employee retention are key to enterprise success. The retention of productive employees is known to be a major human resource challenge, particularly as it becomes increasingly difficult and costly to find and attract skilled people.

In a report from the International Labour Organization (ILO) titled *Women in Business and Management: The business case for change*, almost 13,000 enterprises in 70 countries were surveyed from November 2017 until January 2018. Of the enterprises surveyed, 48 percent experienced retention of skilled women as a challenge for their business, with large enterprises struggling more than small and medium-sized enterprises.[34] Some reasons for this challenge could include maternity leave, recruitment of these women by other enterprises, and female entrepreneurship.

Furthermore, the World Economic Forum report "The Future of Jobs" (2016) says that companies are focusing primarily on progressing women through the pipeline to avoid losing already developed or developing talent.[35] However, few industries are making targeted efforts to hire women into junior and entry-level roles. Across all industries, companies reported that they found women harder to recruit.

Overall, research suggests that the retention of skilled women is challenging for many companies. As such, businesses need to identify factors affecting the retention of female staff, create an inclusive business culture that encourages them to stay, and also draw up initiatives to attract new female talent.

▷ Employer Brand and Recruitment

In the ILO survey, 57 percent of the enterprises that tracked and initiated gender diversity said it was easier to attract and retain talent.[36] Numerous studies reveal the same result: A diverse workforce signals an attractive work environment for talent.

Organizations with a reputation for being a good place for diverse groups to work—gender or otherwise—find it easier to recruit and retain top talent, saving time and money in the long run. Failing to attract the most talented employees has a domino effect on business results. When employers are forced to hire from a dwindling pool, the quality of their hires can drop, initiating a downward spiral of lower productivity and higher costs. As outlined in the Women in Mining

Canada report, managers will generally agree that having the best-qualified hires compared to settling for the same number of mediocre hires translates into a significant difference in productivity.[37]

Manpower Group (2018) reports that employers around the world are struggling to fill job vacancies, with a record high of 45 percent of employers since 2006 saying that they can't find the skills they need. Manpower also notes that there is a considerable gap between the roles that employers offer and the roles women are seeking, which are often positions with more flexible work arrangements. And yet, in 2013, Manpower found that "only 6 percent of shortage-affected employers are redesigning work procedures such as sharing work assignments," while "only 5 percent are offering more flexible work arrangements, and just one employer in fifty provides virtual work options to candidates."

Research has shown that employees in the U.S. and Western Europe prefer diverse work environments. In a survey of 1,000 respondents, the job site Glassdoor found that 67 percent of job seekers overall look at workforce diversity when evaluating an offer.[38] Top female candidates in particular care about gender-diverse work environments.

A recent survey found that 61 percent of women look at the gender diversity of the employer's leadership team when deciding where to work.[39] The takeaway is the most talented individuals go to places that do better with diversity, and this may be what is driving diverse firms in certain contexts to outperform their peers. And imagine if you shifted your procurement policies to include the criteria of including 50 percent of companies that are female led?

Given what I've shared with you thus far, do you think there are benefits to be gained by hiring a female-run supply chain company? I've met many middle-aged engineering women, for example, who are now deciding to run their own businesses to give them greater control not only over their work but also their personal life. They are some of the most dynamic, smart, and efficient people I know.

You can test the waters in your company regarding the benefits of gender diversity and inclusion by simply seeking out supply chain companies that are women-led and see the results for yourself. That just might be the most convincing step you can take to get the wheels in motion.

The Cost of Inaction

Earlier in this section, I mentioned the Rio Declaration of 1992. Well, it was in 1997 that, while working at the environmental engineering firm marketing the firm to the federal government, I was asked if I would like to come and work on the United Nations "Rio +5" file in the federal government. My job was to put on an international exhibit in the lobby of the United Nations General Assembly Special Session in New York, showcasing success stories from around the world on sustainable development over the five years since the Rio Declaration had been made in 1992.

I was also asked to put together a side event with Maurice Strong speaking to the financial district of New York. For those who don't know, Maurice Strong was what I would call the "grandfather of sustainable development." He was at the forefront for the push to create the Rio Declaration that outlined global issues that needed to be brought to the world's attention.

Needless to say, I leapt at the opportunity and was quickly on a fast-track circuit to find funding at the World Bank, the Global Environment Facility, the United Nations Environment Programme, and the United Nations Development Program. Back in those days, you were given far more responsibility at an earlier stage. I was doing this on my own at twenty-six years old.

That year, I flew all over the world, seeking funding and then projects to showcase—Washington, New York, Kenya, Rio, and elsewhere. But it was at home, between trips and in the safe confines of Ottawa, that on a Saturday afternoon, along the historic canal, while speed-walking and wearing my Walkman (remember those?), that I was assaulted.

I didn't hear him approach. I was in the middle of my walk when a young man put his arm over me and grabbed my crotch. For a split-second, I thought, *Who do I know that would do this?* Then I immediately realized *NOBODY I know would do this!*

As I shrugged him off my shoulder and turned around, I could see his other hand down his pants. He took off, and I started running after him.

Although afflicted with asthma, I had warmed up from my walk and became larger than life as I started racing after this guy. In my mind, I could only think, *You've crossed the wrong victim today, pal.* I chased him for just over a block, and he ran behind a house where there was a parking area. I ran up and grabbed him by the scruff of his shirt. It was at that point that *he* yelled, "Don't touch me!" I screamed back at him, "F*%$ you! You touched *me!*"

As I was dragging and pulling him toward the sidewalk, a truck came whizzing around the corner. A woman got out and yelled, "I'm an off-duty police officer, and I saw the chase!" The police officer threw him up against her truck, cuffed him, and took him into custody.

I later learned that this man had assaulted several other women along the canal but had never been caught. He was sentenced to three months in jail, and I hope he learned his lesson. I certainly learned mine—nowhere is sacred.

If this situation could happen to me in one of the nicest countries, in one of the nicest cities, in one of the nicest neighbourhoods, in broad daylight, with cars driving by, it could happen anywhere.

In fact, just about daily, I turn on the news and find some sexual harassment story of a guy using his power to dominate someone, either directly or indirectly. These lawsuits cover the watershed of sectors. Nowhere seems sacred—not even the church. Sports coaches, doctors, members of the military, executives in various organizations, and the world of showbiz have all made the news recently for harassment.

The list of people who have done something completely inappropriate in the workplace seems endless. And I sit there and think, *really*?

Is mankind still operating in the missing link era? How is it that we can build technology that takes us to the moon, but we can't manage to control our behaviour in the workplace?

I currently work closely with the Canadian forest sector, and I have heard stories about guys operating in the bush camps who drank one too many, mistakenly entered a comrade's bunker, and proceeded to pee on his head, thinking he was in the toilet. Again, seriously? (I thought this had to be made up, but the source for this story was someone knowledgeable about these camps, a non-drinker, and I believe him.) Plus, hazing is common in campsites, and from what I've heard about them, they take all the relaxation out of being one with nature.

The point is, these behaviours are unacceptable, and it's time that leaders start setting the ground rules on codes of conduct in the workplace, in head offices and in the camps, to help both women *and* men out to have a healthier workplace. And once these codes of conduct are clearly communicated, people have to be held accountable. The culture of any organization is dictated entirely from the top executive(s), so it's incumbent upon them to create the psychological safety that allows everyone to speak up if conditions are inappropriate.

Again, the value proposition of proceeding with a GDI strategy reaffirms this. In terms of sheer economics, let's consider the following sampling of companies that have been slammed with serious financial repercussions due to poor conduct:

- In 2016, Google paid former search executive Amit Singhal $35 million in an exit package when he was reportedly forced to resign after a sexual assault investigation. Details of the exit package were revealed as part of a shareholder lawsuit against the company that followed a published report of payouts Google made to executives accused of sexual misconduct.[40]
- McDonald's workers in Michigan filed a class-action lawsuit in 2019 that seeks to force the fast-food chain to address a "systemic problem" of sexual harassment across its restaurants. At least 50 McDonald's workers separately filed sexual harassment charges against the company with the U.S. Equal Employment Opportunity Commission (EEOC).[41]
- Four women who worked in the corporate headquarters at Nike filed a class-action lawsuit at a federal court in Oregon in 2018, claiming that Nike violated the Equal Pay Act by engaging in systemic gender pay discrimination and ignored rampant sexual harassment. The lawsuit captures the frustration of multiple women who tried to climb the corporate ladder at Nike, which employs more than 67,000 workers in the United States and around the globe.[42]
- Nearly 100 workers filed gender discrimination lawsuits against Walmart in February of 2019 alleging denial of equal pay for retail store employees and certain salaried management positions. The plaintiffs included current Walmart employees and others who left the company from the early to late 2000s.
- The Federal Court approved a $900-million agreement to settle multiple class-action lawsuits by survivors of sexual harassment

and assault in the Canadian Armed Forces and Department of National Defense.[43]

- A group of more than 700 female nurses working in the federal public service won a $150-million human rights settlement in 2014 after arguing that the government paid them less based on their gender.[44]

- A federal jury in California awarded Ani Chopourian $168 million, potentially the largest judgment in U.S. history for a single victim of workplace sexual harassment, in a case against Catholic Healthcare West.

- In July 2019, the Royal Canadian Mounted Police (RCMP) agreed to cash settlements in response to a lawsuit alleging sexual harassment within its ranks. The federal class-action suit alleges municipal employees, contractors, and volunteers who either worked with or were supervised by the RCMP experienced gender- and sexual orientation-based harassment and discrimination while working for the force. It was estimated that 1,500 women would come forward, and, because claims aren't capped, the settlement could top $100 million in payouts.[45]

- And in 2017 Twenty First Century Fox News paid out $50 million for a sexual harassment lawsuit – and get this – paid the accused males a combined $64 million package to go away.[46] How is it that the guys walked away with more of a cash settlement, and they committed the crime? Enquiring minds want to know!

- Another story near and dear to my heart (because I'm currently working in the forest sector) is news that came out in January 2020 regarding female tree planters who purported that they had experienced sexual harassment in the campsites they work in. I suspect that is not going to go away without any impact, either financially or through workforce retention.

Now honestly, wouldn't it be a whole lot easier to seek a culture in your workplace that avoids these kinds of gong show behaviours?

And let's face it, no GDI strategy will ever cost you millions of dollars to put into action.

Not only is it painful for those on the front lines of these stories, but everyone else who works there feels guilty by association. And the leaders are always going to be the ones who are held accountable.

The good news is that the risk of losing money and credibility due to lawsuits such as these can be mitigated by committing to being a diverse and inclusive company. By proactively implementing training for a safe, respectful, and equal-opportunity workplace across every company tier and demonstrated from the top down, these threats can be eliminated, and companies can be set up to thrive. Creating accountability for behaviour is key.

The point is this is no longer a women's issue. It's an everybody issue.

Another Driver: Legislation

The economic advantages, as outlined above, are pushing leaders to see the benefits of implementing a gender strategy, but we must also consider the pull that is coming from legislation in Canada and around the world. Legislation tends to target the pay gap between men and women but does not venture (yet) into other key aspects that could help the cause, including policies and practices.

In Canada in 2018, a woman earned 87 cents on the dollar as measured in hourly wages for full-time workers.[47] Today in the U.S., on average a woman working full time earns 80.7 cents for every dollar a man working full-time earns. According to data from the U.S. Census Bureau, women's median annual earnings are $9,909 less than those of men. Black and Hispanic women are most affected by the wage gap, especially when compared to white men.[48]

McKinsey Global Institute released a study that mapped fifteen gender equality indicators for 95 countries. The indicators consisted of several categories: equality in work, essential services, enablers of economic opportunity, legal protection, political voice, physical security, and autonomy.[49] Forty of the countries were found to have high or extremely high levels of gender inequality on at least half of the indicators.

A news release issued from the Government of Canada listed multiple underlying causes for the gender wage gap:

- Work traditionally performed by women has historically been undervalued, and a greater share has been unpaid.
- Women are over-represented in part-time, low-paying work.
- Women lack representation in senior positions.
- Bias and discrimination still commonly exist in the workplace.

Changes are afoot, however. A recent news release announced that in Canada, for example, women can count on equal pay for work of equal value. In October 2018, proactive pay equity legislation for the federal jurisdiction was introduced, called an *Act to Establish a Proactive Pay Equity Regime within the Federal Public and Private Sectors*. This legislation affects public servants and the organizations they run, such as transportation facilities like ports and rail. It signals to Canadians that the government of Canada takes this issue seriously and that women are valued for their work.

As outlined in the Government's news release, proactive pay equity legislation is an important tool that will contribute to reducing the gender wage gap, but "it needs to be part of a broader array of policy tools, such as the Government's investments in early learning and child care, improved financial support for training and learning, enhanced parental leave flexibility, pay transparency, the continued appointment of skilled, talented women into leadership positions, and better access to flexible work arrangements."[50]

Other countries are implementing changes in legislation as well. In 2018, the Equality and Anti-Discrimination Ombud Act went into effect in Norway. The purpose of this Act is "to promote equality and prevent discrimination on the basis of gender, pregnancy, leave in connection with childbirth or adoption, care responsibilities,

ethnicity, religion, belief, disability, sexual orientation, gender iden-
tity, gender expression, age or other significant characteristics of
a person."[51]

Iceland even has a government rule requiring large businesses
to be either at least 40 percent women or at least 40 percent men.
In 2016, women accounted for 48 percent of elected representatives in parliament.[52] And as of 2017, for the seventh year running,
Iceland topped the World Economic Forum's survey for gender
equality. Out of 144 countries, Iceland ranked number one in political empowerment among women and number one for closing the
gender income gap.[53]

A 2017 report by Australia's Workplace Gender Equality Agency
details how the country's parental leave policies are designed to
support and protect working parents, both women and men,
around the time of childbirth or adoption of a child and when children are young. And they foster a more equal division of unpaid
care and paid work, thus improving the family work-life balance.
Australia's combined approach to parental leave may help break
down gender stereotypes around unpaid and paid work if taken
by women and men. A supportive workplace culture is key to
increasing the number of fathers who take advantage of parental
leave.[54]

It isn't a catch-all, but legislation that advocates for the safety
of women can go a long way. And I'm referring to not just physical
safety but also psychological safety, meaning people need to feel
that they can speak up when something is amiss in the workplace.

The Centre for Research and Education on Violence Against
Women and Children at the University of Western Ontario has
developed excellent guidelines for employers to learn and understand what to watch for with employees who may be affected by
domestic abuse. People don't often think about domestic violence
issues being brought to work. However, it is an important area
where awareness, policies, and training are critical for building safe
and equitable workplaces. [55]

Women tend to not speak up. Part of what they need to work on is improving their assertiveness skills, which we'll talk about in the next chapter. But when they do finally get the courage to speak up, they need to know that:

- There is a safe space to do so where they will be heard.
- What they have experienced in the workplace will be acted on and not dismissed.
- The situation is taken seriously.
- The perpetrator will be held accountable, if necessary.

I've heard one too many stories where a woman speaks up about harassment from a co-worker or boss, only to have that person moved to another role but remain in the same business. This only serves to make the woman feel uncomfortable at work when she passes him in the office, and soon she is the one forced to look for a new job. Being on the receiving end of harassment is hard enough. Is it really fair or reasonable to suggest that the woman should be the one displaced and sent looking elsewhere for a healthy work environment?

Here's another difficult to believe, yet true, story from 2016. A woman was working in a northern mining camp doing the accounting for the mine site. One day a co-worker came over to her desk and put several hundred dollars down and asked for sex in return. She told her boss, but the guy was allowed to keep working, so she quit.

Because it was a fly-in fly-out situation, there was only one flight for this woman to take home. But it just so happened that the perpetrator was at the end of his work shift, so she ended up on the same flight as a man who had propositioned her for sex. Imagine how she felt, having to face him on that small flight home.

Beyond the discomfort to this woman personally, there's also the corporate cost of turnover, the reputation of the company, and the bad behaviour persisting. All of that translates into wasted dollars that could be back in the till. There are no winners here, except for maybe the one doing the harassing who gets to keep his job in spite of his behaviour.

Now let's take a look at a company that has not only embraced diversity and inclusion as a core aspect of their business, but has also demonstrated through years of tracking and monitoring progress an amazing return on their investment in developing and implementing a GDI strategy. As you read this example, think about how you can emulate their efforts in your own company and how you too can make profits and improve the overall health and well-being of your organization.

 Case Study: Sodexo

Founded in Marseille, France in 1966, Sodexo is the global leader in services that improve quality of life, an essential factor in individual and organizational performance. Operating in 72 countries, Sodexo serves 100 million consumers each day through its unique combination of services. From food services, facilities and equipment management, and programs fostering employee engagement, to concierge services and in-home assistance, the company offers a unique array of solutions that simplify and optimize the way work gets done.

Diversity and inclusion are parts of the brand promise at Sodexo. Their leadership in GDI is critical to helping provide their employees with the best possible work-life experience regardless of age, gender, nationality, culture, race, sexual orientation, or other personal characteristics.

Sodexo's global commitment to diversity and inclusion covers five key dimensions: gender, cultures & origins, disability, LGBTQ, and generations. Within each of these areas, they continue to implement programs and initiatives that foster an inclusive culture and drive change in local communities, while impacting the lives of individuals around the world.

▷ The Results

Initially, Sodexo was struggling to get managers worldwide to buy into diversity initiatives. The company realized that they needed to build a business case for more women in leadership. Sodexo looked at how business units with different proportions of women and men in management performed on a range of key financial and non-financial metrics, including client retention, employee engagement, and workplace safety.

In 2014, an internal study was launched to explore and understand the correlation between gender-balanced management and performance. Part two was released in 2018. They now have over five years of data, covering 50,000 managers in 70 entities worldwide, which suggests that gender-balanced teams outperform those that are not gender-balanced, and the optimal mix of gender is 40 to 60 percent women. Here are some of the study's other results from having implemented gender-balanced teams:

- Employee engagement increased by 14 percentage points.
- Employee retention increased by 8 percentage points.
- Client retention increased by 9 percentage points.
- Safety increased by 12 percentage points.
- Operating margins increased by 8 percentage points.

Sodexo used these results to build a business case for getting more women in management. The company set a goal that 40 percent of senior leaders would be women by 2025. To help meet this goal, 10 percent of annual bonuses for senior leaders is now contingent on making progress against it.[56]

Sodexo's diversity efforts are paying off. With women currently comprising half of the board, 32 percent of the company's senior leaders, and nearly 50 percent of its total workforce, it is among the most gender-diverse companies in its industry group and home country. From 2011 to 2019, Sodexo has had a 66-percent increase in women executives and a 60 percent increase in racially diverse executives. It is also among the most successful companies financially within McKinsey's data set.

The Sodexo Corporation is an example of an organization that has exponentially increased its return on investment through GDI initiatives. According to Dr. Rohini Anand, the company's senior vice president and global chief diversity officer, for every $1 it has invested in mentoring, it has seen a return of $19.[57] When considering the facts, the value proposition of gender-diverse work environments can't be ignored.

My Introduction to Working in GDI

When I was twenty-eight, I applied for a program through the government of Canada that selected thirty Canadians under the age of thirty who were unemployed or felt they were underemployed.

I identified as underemployed, meaning there was a certain qualification I didn't have but needed to get the job I really wanted. That qualification was a work placement in a developing country.

I had my sights set on working at the Canadian International Development Agency (now Global Affairs Canada), and this was my ticket to getting there. I was thrilled when I was selected and subsequently daunted by the placement location: New Delhi, India.

This was 1999. The internet was just making its way into offices in Canada, but access to it in India was hit or miss, meaning that communication back home would be sparse at best.

It was a big deal as a white-skinned, blue-eyed female to go to a culture I knew nothing about for a minimum of six months. And it proved to be an education on many levels. As a young woman, I would walk to work at the Tata Energy Research Institute (TERI), and three guys would walk backwards just two feet ahead of me, staring at me as I made my way down the street for three blocks. It was over the top. I felt like I lived in a fishbowl. This happened a couple of times, and then one day, I'd had enough. I spoke up to them and said, "Have you never seen a white woman before?" They seemed shocked that I could speak. I didn't see them again after that. This would be one of my early lessons on finding my voice.

TERI was at that time (and perhaps still is) the most prestigious Non-Government Organization (NGO) in India on energy issues. I was tasked with doing research on developing India's climate change strategy. When I look back now, these were the beginning years for developing ideas for what India would be doing on the international stage.

I was familiar with the climate change file, having been asked to stay on another year in government to work on the lead up to the famous "Kyoto Protocol" after the "Rio+5" file was complete. But at that time, the world was struggling to figure out how to meet greenhouse gas emission targets in developing countries. And any and all greenhouse gas (ghg) emission targets seemed out of reach and unrealistic.

At the same time, a colleague I knew from Ontario Hydro (now Ontario Power Generation) found out I was in India. The company was looking to start a pilot project in India that would provide a real-case example of how to write the rules on what was called the "clean development mechanism." This referred to an emissions trading scheme between a developed and developing country.

I was excited; it was a project I wanted to support. At the time, the Prime Minister of India had implemented a one million well program. He literally had a million water wells dug around the country, but there was no way to access the water, so the wells were useless for all intents and purposes. They needed a means of getting the water to the land. So, I found a company that specialized in solar-powered water pumps that was looking for an investor. It was perfect. It had the environmental solution (using solar panels) to pump water to the land to grow vegetables (creating jobs) that could then be sold (boosting the economy). It met the criteria of environmental, social, and economic benefits, and Ontario Hydro loved it.

We made the deal happen, and it was extremely exciting. The process for that project was captured and subsequently shared with the United Nations Framework Convention on Climate Change (UNFCCC) to help guide them write the rules on the Clean Development Mechanism.

While in India I decided to apply for my master's degree in International Environment, Development, and Policy at the University of Sussex in England. I had no idea how I would pay for such an expensive school, but I figured I'd worry about that if or when I was accepted. At that point, it was a bit like watching the universe unfolding before my eyes almost effortlessly. That same week, I found out that a side contract for Ontario Power Generation, which I had completed on the margins of working at TERI, proved to be quite lucrative. When the acceptance letter to Sussex came in later the same week, I knew I wasn't in charge of my destiny. I merely had to keep doing what I was doing. A path was already carved out for what I was to do next with my life.

I was blessed with a great early career that carried on with exciting files and exposure to international people and venues. I was constantly curious to learn more and wanted to figure out how to make things better, improve current systems, and elevate thinking and behaviours to get people working collaboratively on important issues.

Taking Action on Gender Diversity and Inclusion

In the early days of turning my mind toward gender equality issues, Women in Mining Canada asked me to write a proposal for a grant opportunity with a federal government department called the Status of Women Canada (now Women and Gender Equality).

I knew a little about the mining sector from my degrees and my policy and environmental assessment work, but that was entirely from an economic and environmental point of view. I certainly didn't know anything about gender equality at the time, but I knew how to write proposals. So I said, "Sure, I can do that. What's the deadline?" She said it was that Friday, giving me only seven days to come up with an idea, get as many letters of support from mining companies and organizations as I could, conduct the research, and write the grant proposal. But I got it done.

Several months later, I found out that we had secured the funding. When they asked if I would like to run the project, I said yes.

I was used to managing projects, so that part wasn't an issue for me. However, I had to start delving deep into the research on the topic to get familiar with the issues and, of course, how it affected that sector in particular.

The biggest challenge I faced was getting mining companies to sit on my steering committee. Not only was this a time when gender equality was not on the radar of Canadians in general, but the mining sector was also experiencing a downturn. The private sector, in particular, had no motivation or interest in even entertaining the discussion.

Ultimately, I did end up recruiting many committed women and a couple of men to steer the action plan from ideation to implementation. These visionary committee members helped guide this project by shining a light on gender inequality in the mining sector. They created awareness at the sector level, but, as part of this committee, they were also tasked with implementing changes within their own companies.

These individuals became the gender equality champions in their companies at a time when nobody cared to listen. It was a different way of doing business for these folks. They normally competed with each other, now they were united in their effort to create change on gender equality in their sector.

The purpose of the project was to get more women in the mining sector in senior executive roles and technical positions and to create a team of gender champions in the mining sector to work collaboratively and look at barriers and best practices. They defined actions to affect change on gender equality in the workplace, and that action plan has since become a useful guide for governments and organizations in South America and elsewhere.

On the heels of the mining sector action plan wrapping up, I was approached by the forest sector to do something similar. I took the knowledge I gained in mining and went much deeper and broader in scope and impact on gender diversity and inclusion. I was able to secure greater funding for the forest sector and sought out a not-for-profit partner, the Canadian Institute of Forestry, to be the face of the project in that sector. Together, we created a gender champions steering committee comprised of 60/40 women-to-men ratio of private, public, not-for-profit, academic, and Indigenous representatives from across the sector.

This project is still ongoing, and as was the case with mining, it's important to recognize that these sectors are science and engineering based. The number of women in Science Technology Engineering and Math (STEM) fields is low relative to other sectors. Put another way, we were making a big impact in a sector that was arguably the least likely to deviate from its "business as usual" workplace culture.

With this forest sector committee, we have created a new vision for the sector with a focus on gender equality, articulating the business case and engaging men as part of the solution. This exciting three-year project (2018-21) will move the sector from "laggards to leaders" and has already harnessed amazing energy and momentum among the committee members. Each member is learning new tools, approaches, knowledge and making contacts across the sector that help them become the go-to gender champions of the sector. It's a unified front. With all stakeholders working hand in hand, this project will create a wave of change in a short period of time.

I believe that approaching a gender diversity and inclusion culture shift on a sector-wide basis with key stakeholders is a highly effective way to realize results quickly. In fact, when you look up the United Nations Beijing Declaration and Platform for Action from 1995, this approach of bringing together all stakeholders across a sector is what they asked countries to do! I am excited to share that I am now being asked to consider working in other sectors to help them in this effort. Under my business, Centre for Social Intelligence, the scope of each project continues to expand and move the yardstick one step closer to gender equality in the workplace.

Companies that prioritize building gender-balanced and inclusive teams set themselves up for giant competitive advantages. Not only is it economically and socially advantageous, but diversity and inclusion represent the evolution of the workforce. This is how leadership should be moving forward. If those in the C-suite ignore the facts, their companies will be left behind.

It's time to get on board with what successful companies have already figured out. It's time to lead the change.

Takeaways

The statements below summarize the main points you can take away from this chapter.

- The cost-benefit analysis of implementing a gender diversity and inclusion strategy shows greater returns than if nothing was in place.
- The potential liability of an employee or peer who decides to engage in inappropriate behaviour in the workplace can be extremely costly.
- The economic benefits will pull you, and the legislation will push you toward action on gender diversity and inclusion.
- Turnover of employees will decrease—for women *and* for men.
- Gender equality will create:
  ◇ Increased profitability and productivity
  ◇ An enhanced ability to attract and retain talent
  ◇ Greater creativity, innovation, and openness
  ◇ An enhanced company reputation
  ◇ Better ability to gauge consumer interest demand

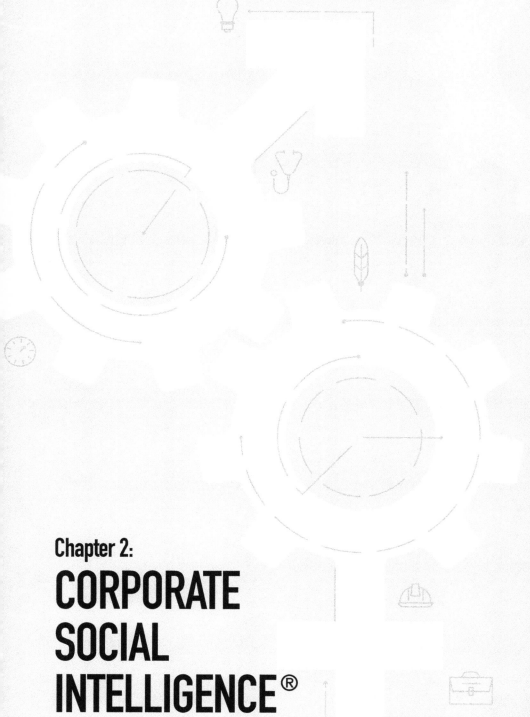

Chapter 2:
CORPORATE
SOCIAL
INTELLIGENCE®

C orporate values are often created as part of an image a company wishes to convey, either internally or externally. But when you scratch the surface, they are not so often upheld.

I recently spoke with the president of a progressive company and asked if diversity and inclusion was a part of his company values. He responded, "Values don't really mean anything." I was shocked he would be so brazen, yet not all that surprised by his answer. Although a true admission on his part, it speaks to the root problem of company cultures.

I can't help but think that if you had values that essentially were your code of conduct, and you put a firm boundary around them for all employees to clearly understand and abide by, you would create a safe space. People would feel they could trust the organization to have their backs. I believe this safe space, both emotional and physical, contributes to the intangible stuff that translate into higher performance and innovation.

Think about this in the context of your own home. I did this recently with my family. My kids were entering their teenage years, and respectful behaviour was starting to wane a bit, not just with us parents (think management), but also among the siblings (think peers). I decided one day to put up a Household Code of Conduct on the fridge. It simply stated things like:

- I will be honest with my family.

- I will respect my elders.
- I will be engaged with those in this house.
- I will ask questions and listen when I'm confused about the next steps.
- I will be patient and not take others for granted.
- I will apologize when I know I have wronged someone.
- I will trust that my family supports me.
- I will contribute to the larger good.
- I will be accountable for my words and actions.

I brought these "commandments" to the kids' attention at dinner and asked them if these were reasonable requests for them to abide by. They agreed they were. I was making them accountable for their words and actions. Whenever I saw behaviour that slipped off the edges of these principles, I reminded them that they were a part of this family, and this was how we were to treat each other. It took a few reminders, but change did take place.

Emotional and Social Intelligence

Many behavioural codes of conduct come from emotional intelligence teachings. In his 1995 book *Emotional Intelligence*, Daniel Goleman popularized the concept of emotional intelligence (EI) and asserted that EI surpasses IQ as a determinant of workplace success. EI has since emerged as a critical factor in workplace success for individuals and leaders, as well as for teams.

Diversity enriches an organization's ability to respond to its customers or other stakeholders with more creative and more innovative products and solutions. Yet to fully embrace the diverse backgrounds, intellects, and cultural perspectives within an organization, individual employees and leaders must apply EI to building, maintaining, and leveraging relationships.

EI encompasses interdependent competencies in both self-awareness (i.e., managing our own emotions appropriately and productively) and responsiveness to others (accurate empathetic perceptions of others' feelings, appropriate responses to those emotions with empathy, and managing or assisting others in managing their emotional responses). As recognized by Goleman and his colleagues, "Organizations that embrace diversity, weave the notion of inclusion into their cultures, and align diversity work with their strategies have an increased likelihood of performing to their full potential. Diverse workforces can bring a wider variety of intellectual power and life experience to support the challenge of creating innovative solutions and products."[58]

Human beings function on rational and emotional levels, but emotions are at the heart of our energy, commitment, and motivation. Feelings are also key in forming our reactions to the differences that we perceive in ourselves and others.

Emotions determine whether people accept, reject, approach, avoid, or engage with others. The more we understand and manage emotional responses, the more we enjoy greater comfort in relationships and interactions, and the more we experience social effectiveness and inner peace. Wherever people interact, especially in the workplace, differences in values, languages, behaviours, preferences, and norms occur. Whether these differences seem familiar or unfamiliar, intriguing or confusing, frustrating or fun, or desirable or not; they get to the core of an individual's intellectual and emotional responses. Emotional reactions lead to behaviours that can be effective or ineffective, depending on each individual's ability to deal properly with their feelings.

The EI needed to cope effectively in a diverse and inclusive world involves insight and action, and it requires an effort to improve both oneself and our interactions with others.

I believe we are on the cusp of a paradigm shift in the workplace culture. As we shed light on the need for EI skills development within ourselves and recognize the benefits of it as it applies to diversity and inclusion, people will emerge better off for themselves and their corporate entities. It leads to greater collaboration, acceptance, understanding, and performance.

Stemming from the concept of EI and its connection to diversity and inclusion, I assert that we need social intelligence in our workplace, meaning the corporate culture must tie EI competencies to corporate values. By doing so, the social intelligence of the organization is improved. Improvements can be seen in the form of a more innovative and dynamic workplace; greater retention of staff; and improved motivation, loyalty, respect, and trust. These intangible improvements are hard to quantify but are key to creating a sense of belonging. And when people feel they belong, they excel.

When I first struck up my consulting business, I took the psychology term "social intelligence" and applied it to the corporate world. I defined it as follows:

> Corporate SOCIAL INTELLIGENCE® is when an organization acknowledges, addresses, and invests in the social dimensions of an organization, such as gender diversity and inclusion, mental health, and intergenerational issues with the goal of increasing productivity, health and wellness, and the bottom line. This is achieved by giving individuals in an organization the necessary tools and skills to develop themselves to create a healthy and sustainable work environment for all.

I consider corporate social intelligence to include a suite of EI skills, including self-awareness, self-governance, empathy, impulse control, and assertiveness. I believe that having social intelligence as a value that captures these EI skills and educating all employees to have them as part of their core competency will improve acceptance of diversity and inclusion across any organization.

All people, regardless of gender, race, or religion, have the capacity to realize their potential, creating benefits for themselves and their company. The corporate social intelligence (CSI) system is based on respect for oneself and others and accountability for one's behaviour. A shift along these lines can be achieved through CSI training—zeroing in specifically on how these values apply to gender diversity and inclusion. So, let's get started.

Corporate Social Intelligence Skills

I'd like you to reflect on how you react to things like:

- You hear ethnic or racial slurs or jokes from people who defend their behaviour by saying, "We can't have fun around here anymore now that we have to be so politically correct."
- Diversity and inclusion is weakened because eyes roll and it's seen as the "flavour of the month."
- Your input is not sought out, or your suggestions are sidelined because of your age, gender, education, and/or experience.
- Executives give verbal support for diversity and inclusion but can't seem to move it forward by giving it the necessary resources, both human and financial, to get on with implementation.

These circumstances evoke emotional responses like anger, disappointment, and frustration and really get your blood boiling. But if we flip it around and focus on improving our EI capabilities, turning our emotions from negative to positive ones, we can improve our emotional responses and turn our communication and engagement to constructive paths toward diversity and inclusion, such as improved creativity and innovation. Developing the capacity to understand others and manage our reactions toward them, no matter how great the differences, is a critical competency in the workplace and essential to professional success.

Our colleagues nowadays speak multiple languages, cover several generations, and include many ethnicities and races. They have different personalities, sexual orientations, and religions. Therefore, it's critical that we learn how to embrace and value differences. But how well that is done is based in large part on EI capabilities. If corporate social intelligence is embraced by key stakeholders throughout a company, yet you choose to put your head in the sand and not practice these skills as an individual or leader, you may find that you've been left behind and will soon be shown the door.

Self-Awareness

Have you ever wondered why you repeat certain behaviours that you promised yourself or others you would stop doing? Are you aware that you feel more comfortable reporting to one gender versus another, or one ethnicity versus another? Can you recall a time when you reacted emotionally when someone asked where you were from or how you got your job?

Self-awareness is the ability to take an honest look at yourself in a non-judgemental way and with a sense of curiosity. It stimulates insights into how you think and act and can show you your strengths and vulnerabilities.

A check-in on your own behaviours, feelings, and intentions is a fundamental step in choosing a better and more effective means of communicating with colleagues, managing your emotions, and accepting others. And unlike IQ, the beauty of EI skills is that anyone can develop them. Nobody is born with these skills already in their DNA. It requires your parents, family, and bosses modelling the behaviour and developing your own introspective skills.

Self-awareness is the skill that allows you to realize that you can only control yourself and your reactions to others; you can't control others. It is also the first step in impulse control, which I will discuss later in this chapter.

Being comfortable with yourself and knowing what motivates you, what frustrates you, and what influences you helps you better understand who you are. This is key to becoming accepting and valuing others. Stereotypes, biases, and hot buttons reflect the opinions, beliefs, and knee-jerk reactions that we all have but are often too embarrassed to acknowledge. But any of these emotions or beliefs can create strong feelings and reactions.

Can you remember a time when you interviewed a woman and thought she wasn't speaking up enough? A belief that everyone should be forthright and vocal can cause some people to stereotype that woman as being shy.

We also must be aware that we can trigger others' biases or stereotypes. Personally, I have had many times where people questioned my capabilities based on my looks. One of my first bosses told me jokingly that it would be better for me if I wore a garbage bag and no make-up because the male-dominated sector I was working in might find me attractive and not take me seriously. That was definitely a "wow—seriously?" sort of moment.

And what about ageism? Some people who are in their early fifties already feel overlooked by their bosses because of the focus we have on millennials and youth in general. These folks still have many years of working careers ahead of them and want to step into leadership roles to broaden their horizons, yet they are often ignored. By being aware of these issues, we are now open to seeing things differently, and this ultimately affects our decision-making.

As corporate culture continues to become a melting pot of leaders and employees from various gender identifications, regions, cultural backgrounds, shared values, languages, and behaviours; and norms cannot be assumed. It is becoming all more imperative that team members understand and respect the emotions of others in the workplace in an effort to successfully manage increased diversity.

A 2016 article by Umamaheswararao Jada, et al titled "Emotional Intelligence, Diversity, and Organizational Performance: Linkages and Theoretical Approaches for an Emerging Field" brings this case to point. The authors write, "We hypothesize that if organizations are able to hire employees with good [EI] skills, it would create smooth functioning of a team, otherwise the employed personnel should be trained properly in EI to accept challenges during workforce diversity." This is a fancy way of saying they hire for EI skills when affecting change on gender diversity and inclusion, and if the person doesn't have those skills, they make sure the hired individual is trained to deal effectively with their diverse workforce.

Here's an example. John grew up in a traditional household. His father worked, and his mother was a stay-at-home mom. John married, and, although his wife worked initially, once they had children, she stayed home to raise the kids. John moved up the ladder in his career and was able to travel for work, work later hours as needed, and become quite successful. His self-image was closely tied to his career, and he liked that. He liked being the breadwinner and providing for his family. Other than administrative support roles, John only had men reporting directly to him. Their work styles were similar to his, never turning down travel requirements and working late hours whenever required.

One day, John's direct report Bill came to him and said he had a highly capable woman named Grace working for him. Grace was exceptional with the technical aspects of her work and also seemed to be able to motivate those in her team to do their best. She had been there for a few years and had proven herself time and again, so when she asked Bill if she could change her work schedule to accommodate childcare needs and compress her days into four-day workweeks instead of five, Bill didn't hesitate to support her. After all, she works hard and always delivers. In fact, Bill would argue that she could do the a full day's work in just half the time. So, Bill went to John and put Grace's request forward.

"No," said John. "If I let her do that, everyone is going to start slacking off and asking for a compressed workweek."

Bill countered by saying that everyone knew Grace and her circumstances with her childcare needs. None of them would see this as Grace taking advantage of the situation. It was just that she couldn't adjust her childcare right now.

John dug his heels in saying, "When she's prepared to make work her priority, she can always have a job waiting for her. But it seems her kids take precedence right now. Best to find a replacement for her. And you should probably make it a man so that this situation doesn't happen again."

John lacks self-awareness. He neglected to consider that not everyone comes from an upbringing like his, where his mother and his wife stayed home to raise the kids. John had a particular lens through which he looked at home life and family care. If he had recognized that he may have been raised in ways that are not always the norm for younger generations, John could have created an equitable situation for Grace by helping her out and retaining a dedicated and committed worker. Losing Grace also meant losing her accumulated tribal knowledge, as she had been there for several years. Letting Grace go means that Bill will have to reinvest significant time through the hiring process and while onboarding another person all over again, costing the company money and losing the healthy relationships that were already in place with Grace.

There are many self-awareness moments that. When we stop and think through where our bias and stereotypes come from, we can untangle how we got them in the first place and look at life from another person's perspective. In this instance, John could have said, "Yeah, I don't know how Grace does it. She works hard, is always on time, and seems to create a great team environment around her. She's got her hands full with juggling kids too! Let's be sure to tell others that she is still delivering her fair share of work and that the situation is temporary so there are no misunderstandings, and then let's adjust her schedule to support her."

That decision by John would allow Bill to support Grace and maintain a good working relationship. It would also help John and Bill by not having to go through a search for a new employee. Furthermore, it's an opportunity for John, as the leader, to demonstrate that he has his employee's back. And, of course, it would help Grace, who would be thankful enough to quickly get childcare arrangements up and running as soon as possible to return to a five-day workweek.

Individuals with a strong sense of self-awareness recognize when they feel out of sorts, irritable, or sad. They perceive when these feelings alter their behaviour in ways that might alienate others. Usually, they can also figure out what incident precipitated their feelings. The capacity to know what they are feeling and how they are behaving allows them a degree of control over their potentially alienating behaviour.

Self-Governance

Aristotle once said, "Knowing thyself is the beginning of all wisdom," and I couldn't agree more.

Self-awareness helps us uncover all the imprinting that has shaped who we have become. But then, when we enter the work world, all of that imprinting can get challenged by the new experiences we have and the new people we meet. In the context of this book, self-awareness is challenged by differences in ethnicity, culture, and gender. Destructive or counterproductive behaviours sometimes emerge when differences trigger powerful feelings.

Self-awareness helps people understand why differences trigger emotional reactions, but self-governance is the process of making choices to channel those emotions *into positive and productive behaviours*, versus negative and counterproductive behaviours toward ourselves and others.

Being able to master feelings evoked by differences and being comfortable with the ambiguity that comes from being a part of a diverse environment is key to self-governance. Being flexible and adaptable in the face of change is also essential.

Personal differences can trigger negative self-talk. For example, a man might look at a woman and think, *She is so feminine, how could she possibly do this job?* It's up to us to "turn the channel" on the kind of unhelpful messages that are sometimes triggered by dealing with certain people.

As I touched upon earlier, I left for Africa when I was twenty-two years old on a quest to be one with all things nature. That was my driver. But what ended up happening is that I became a culture junkie. I got the "travel bug" and developed an insatiable curiosity to learn about other cultures.

From Africa, I went to Guatemala, where I stayed with a local family for a month and learned Spanish. I went to the Arctic and learned about the Inuit. Anytime there was an opportunity, I would travel again just to see what the differences were, to learn different ways of achieving similar outcomes, be it related to work or life. My travels helped shape who I am today, my openness to new ideas, my desire to learn about others and their cultures, and my constant desire to seek out how I can better myself using what I learned from them. A healthy curiosity for others is a key component to opening our minds to differences.

Self-governance involves the ability to recognize when a difference, combined with an irrational belief, leads to a destructive emotional consequence. Studies conducted on the impact of intolerance show the importance of overcoming rigid personality traits and the need for governing emotions in times of uncertainty.[59] I've seen this type of scenario show up in the workplace.

A woman in her late thirties (Let's call her Sharon.) is assigned as a director and has a man reporting to her who is in his early fifties (Let's call him Dan). Dan balks at the thought of having to report to someone younger than he is, let alone a female.

As the leader of the group, Sharon wants the team to gel, so she proposes some EI training to help everyone understand themselves better and get to know those they work with. Everyone signs up for the training except Dan. When Sharon approaches Dan about signing up, he says, "I don't need it. I'm not going to be around here beyond five years, and it's just a waste of my time and the company's money."

Clearly, Dan needs training. His self-governance is not in the "positive reaction to change" category. He has blinders on and can't even see how he's coming across. Dan could benefit from learning how his emotional reaction to having a younger female boss isn't working for him. Perhaps he could go deeper and figure out why he's reacting badly. Is it because of a perception of women's roles that he's grown up with? Is it because he thought *he* should have been the one to be the director and now feels overlooked?

If Dan could get to the root of his negative reaction, he could openly share it with his boss and find a positive path forward. If the reason is that he wanted the job, then perhaps there's a way to have Dan be her second in command on certain projects. He may not get the title of director, but he could perhaps get the title of deputy director. And although this may not come with additional money, it could come with additional exposure to senior management. At a minimum, it will improve understanding and communications between Sharon and Dan as they work together in the remaining years of his career. Of course, Dan may not choose to share the root cause of his views, but he may dial in to why he reacted the way he did and respond with more EQ in future.

Once you know what bothers you and why, you then need to be able to direct the energy of your emotional response in a way that is constructive. What emotions come up when:

- You can't make yourself understood because no one speaks your language?
- People discount you because of your ethnicity, age, or gender?
- Someone makes incorrect assumptions about you based on stereotypes?
- You perceive that someone has been discriminated against because of their sexual orientation, accent, or appearance?

Do you feel frustrated, confused, angry, deflated, or diminished? Chances are, one of those emotions surfaces for you. These scenarios play out regularly in the workplace, and yet we wonder why teams aren't gelling.

We want to know how to create high-performing teams through diversity and inclusion, stimulate innovation, and get the return on our social investment; but we struggle to figure it out. By having employees become aware of their own emotions and their triggers to those emotions, they can then take steps to course-correct in a positive direction, which ultimately leads to better relations among the team, spurring innovation and creativity.

Empathy

There are a lot of egocentric people in the work world who are driven to succeed no matter whose back they are stepping on to get there.

I've grown up with and worked with many of them. They are all about themselves and have little time or interest in getting to know you or your circumstances, especially if it gets in the way of them making a buck. Social media isn't helping matters either. People want to post photos of themselves and are keenly aware of how many likes they get. These folks often lack empathy, the ability to see through the eyes of someone else.

Steven Stein, PhD and author of *The EQ Edge: Emotional Intelligence and Your Success*, defines empathy as "the ability to be aware of, understand, and appreciate the feelings and thoughts of others. Empathy is being "tuned in to what, how, and why people feel and think the way they do."[60] By being empathetic, you can shift a difficult conversation into a collaborative one.

Empathy is a key skill for addressing gender diversity and inclusion in the workplace. Like self-awareness and self-governance, empathy is yet another tool in the toolbox to bolster one's ability to generate higher productivity and innovation, making it a skill well worth developing.

It might seem odd at first—achieving productivity via empathy? What a leap in logic. But when you understand that the EQ skills are a make-or-break skill set that separates good companies from great ones, you realize that empathy allows people to truly be heard and understood and leads to a sense of belonging and emotional and physical safety. When people have that sense of comfort, knowing that their colleagues have their backs and their boss understands their circumstances—whether that includes childcare needs, parental care, or ethnic holidays—they are able to create a trusting relationship and stay better focused at work.

One of the other very cool things that comes from empathy is that those who are shown empathy will pass it on to others. For example, if a boss extends empathy and understanding toward an employee, that employee is likely to pass on that same behaviour to his or her staff.

That's the beauty of EQ skills; everyone can learn them. And sometimes, people just need a little guidance toward learning them by having them modelled so they can learn more easily.

When someone doesn't feel secure in their work environment, the front brain is working on the task at hand while the back brain is engaged in negative self-talk, thinking *I can't work with these people. They don't understand me.* An employee may also waste a portion of their productivity time talking with others about how disconnected they feel or searching for a new job where they hope they'll be a better fit. Sound familiar? Here's an example to help illustrate empathy in the workplace.

It was the morning of a big sales presentation, and Dave's daughter had been ill the night before. As a result, he was unable to put together some of the last minute details in time for his co-worker Sarah, who was the lead presenter. Sarah was fuming when Dave revealed that he hadn't yet finished his part. He'd spent hours in the emergency ward the night before, waiting for his daughter to be seen, but the first words out of Sarah's mouth were, "I hate it when you don't pull your weight. If I had known I couldn't depend on you, I would have worked with Jo. Now I'll have to spend the rest of the morning finishing your work. I already had other things I was planning to do for this presentation. Did you even think about how this would impact me?"

Dave could have gotten defensive and retorted, "Well, for your information, I had an emergency last night. I had to take my daughter to the hospital!"

Luckily, Dave was empathetic and said instead, "I'm sorry I don't have the numbers. It must seem to you that I'm not taking this seriously, and you must be frustrated that I haven't kept my commitment to you."

"That's right," Sarah replied, happy he understood. "That's just how I feel. So, what happened? Why don't you have your part worked out?"

Dave's empathetic comment—putting into words Sarah's feelings of frustration and anger—helped to calm her down and shifted the adversarial tone of their relationship to a much more collaborative one. With this new cooperative tone, Sarah was now willing to hear his reason for not doing his work, without perceiving it as an excuse. When she heard that Dave's daughter was in the hospital, her frustration immediately dissipated, and she responded with an apology for her reaction, followed by an explanation about why she was so upset. She really doesn't like to be behind on projects.

Whether it's the janitor, your employee, or your boss, do you take time to listen to what others are telling you? Do you try to understand what they're saying before you jump in? Even if you don't agree with that person's point of view, it doesn't matter. What you're doing is demonstrating that you have heard what it is they are telling you. When you articulate in your own words what you have heard, you can also respond with the context to help reach common ground.

In the example of Dave and Sarah, the context could be that time was in short supply in the first place, so when life events creep in, it's going to be tough to meet fast turnaround deadlines. If you can be empathetic, like Dave, not only will you have heard the other person, but you will have also provided some further information that justifies the difficult situation both of you find yourselves in. Now, you're operating as a team.

Impulse Control

Sometimes, we have impulsive moments. Even when we have the presence of mind to think *I shouldn't do this.* (eating that piece of cake, for example), there are times when we just can't resist. We act on the desire with some awareness of the consequence(s). But, more often than not, people are working without a sense of self-awareness for their impulsive decision. Instead, they just act.

Every day, it seems there is at least one story in the news of someone who has seriously mismanaged an impulse to do something. Such stories sometimes include men who are caught being voyeurs of women, groping someone, or making inappropriate comments. In the workplace, this is when people, like the boss in the back of the taxi who can't keep his hands to himself or the peer who can't resist making a racial slur in the office, can find themselves in a whole heap of trouble. Once something like that happens, it's hard to pull back and save face.

To be clear, men are not the only source of the problem here. I've heard inappropriate comments from women about women, many of which stem solely from jealousy. The attitude of "I had to work hard to get here, so she has to work hard too," is almost like a syndrome. Another inappropriate comment is to claim that a female co-worker is playing the role of a male boss's "work-wife," implying there are some hidden dynamics at play and casting serious doubt in the eyes of others regarding that women's capabilities.

According to Steven Stein, impulse control is "the ability to resist or delay an impulse, drive, or temptation to act. It entails avoiding rash behaviours and decision-making, being composed and able to put the brakes on angry, aggressive, hostile and irresponsible behaviour."

Impulsive people are often the "Act now; think later." Type people. Impulsive people are described as impatient, mercurial, unpredictable, rash, or hot-headed. They have a low tolerance for frustration, can get carried away in the moment, lose sight of the big picture, or fear the unknown (as is the case with cultural differences).

But there's good news. It is possible to learn how to manage one's impulses.

Those who can manage their impulses give themselves the mental space to weigh alternatives and assess options so that their actions and expressions are reasoned and well considered. This leads to wise decision-making and responsible behaviour. Plans made after a period of reflection often have a greater chance of success or, in the context of the GDI, have a greater chance of not making a fool out of you. Many a gender blooper or racial slur could have been avoided if a sober second of thought had been given before speaking.

In the context of gender diversity and inclusion, impulse control is often needed to resist the temptation to judge the behaviour of others according to one's own cultural standards. We must turn impulsive comments around and see the advantages of cultural differences. Different doesn't mean wrong. At the very minimum, people need a safe space to understand differences.

By learning to tolerate uncertainty and the unfamiliar better, one can increase the capacity for teamwork and creativity. One can achieve this environment by fostering an environment of curiosity for other cultures, norms, and values; creating open communication for learning about cultural differences; and recognizing that divergent views bring greater ingenuity and innovation.

Companies that wish to address impulsive behaviours in their employees can conduct training that embraces differences in style, priorities, viewpoints, motivations, and talents. This can go a long way in reducing the number of D&I incidences or impulsive outbursts.

Assertiveness

Assertive people express their feelings and beliefs, often directly, and they can do so without being aggressive or abusive. According to Steven Stein and Howard Book in their book *The EQ Edge*, there are three aspects to being assertive:

- The ability to express feelings (e.g. warmth, anger, frustration)
- The ability to voice opinions, or take a stand even if it's difficult to do so
- The ability to stand up for personal rights (i.e. not let others take advantage of you).

Usually, women are singled out for not being assertive enough or speaking up in general, let alone speaking up for themselves. Meanwhile, women who do speak up are often labelled as aggressive, which becomes a tough line to walk. I jokingly refer to these women as being "passionate aggressive." If you can view women as being passionate about whatever they're speaking about, instead of seeing them as aggressive, chances are you will receive their message more easily and understand them more fully.

I can recall a time when I was consulting for the federal government. There was a man also consulting for the same person. We had two distinct roles. His was focused on performance management, and mine was focused on change management. I was asked to write a change management plan, not just for one department's change on a particular IT initiative, but in conjunction with over eight federal departments. I was told, "Just go home and write it up tomorrow so we can get this moving forward."

Anyone who knows anything about change management knows you cannot just steal away on your own and write a change management plan by yourself. It requires involvement from the executive sponsor, as well as many other stakeholders who will be affected. It was a big task, and it would take many months to implement. The disconnect on the scope of work was hard enough to clarify with the person I reported to. But when I learned that the man who was consulting on performance management was being paid *double* what I was being paid, I had to sit back and think how to engage with my client.

Here I was, fully qualified with a master's degree and over twenty years' experience, getting paid half of what my colleague was being paid. I know the tasks were different, but both tasks at hand required knowledge, skill, and experience, and were equally key to a successful outcome for the project overall. When I heard about the pay difference, I felt I had to speak up because it seemed a grossly unfair situation.

I went to the person I reported to and pointed this difference out. He came back with, "Yeah, but Jeff calls me at all hours in the evening to sort issues out. He's working all the time."

I replied, "I'd be happy to call you at night with work-related issues that need sorting out, but I'm pretty sure your wife wouldn't be comfortable with that."

It was like I had hit him with both barrels right between the eyes. A lightbulb came on, and he had nothing to say. At the next pay period, I was granted the same pay as my colleague.

In this scenario, I had to be clear and logical, which is best for any discussion, but I also had to have confidence that I was of equal value. The younger women in that office wrote me a card when my contract was finished. It read, "Thank you for speaking up with these guys. You've been a great role model, and I'm grateful for having worked with you."

I was touched, and it made me realize that not only had I done something good for myself by being assertive, but there were others watching and benefiting too.

When it comes to being assertive, however, I'm talking about men being assertive too. Men should speak up for women and their rights, advocate for a safe space to speak up, and demand GDI measures that support equality.

In his book, *The Time Has Come: Why Men Must Join the Gender Equality Revolution*, Michael Kaufman describes how our traditional ideals about manhood emerge from and reinforce the realities of a male-dominated society. From an early age, boys and girls are talked to differently, dressed in different clothes, and given different toys. In other words, children are conditioned to follow society's definition of what it means to be a boy or a girl.

Traditionally—and still today to a large extent—boys have been raised to be strong and willful, whereas girls are expected to be gentle, delicate, emotional, and compliant. These gender expectations have been instilled in us over time, having originated from male-dominated societies, religious authorities, all-male government bodies, and even men's sports clubs. Men created and justified the rules governing manhood and womanhood and made sure that those who deviated from those rules were penalized.

These rules are not only detrimental to women. Men are also expected to be perfectly strong, courageous, and without fault at all times. They are to provide; they are to be rugged, hardy, and without need for assistance from anyone at any time. No man can live up to this. Men can't always be strong and fearless, have all the answers, be the economic provider, be ready and able to fight, and yet limit their emotions to anger alone.

Kaufman states, "Male-dominated societies have created expectations and ideals for men that set boys and men up for failure."[61] Men have a huge stake in bringing those traditional beliefs, ideals, and expectations to an end. Some men have come to realize that the real values of human life are not money or power but are relationships with those we love.

Generally, assertiveness has been a skill that most women need to work on to help them speak up and fit in with the mostly male work environment. I believe that focus is important. However, I think there is also a need to include men too—to help support them to be less aggressive and more assertive, to give them a way to speak up for women, challenge the norms, and take a stand for gender equality.

I recently attended a conference and met a couple of men who were very keen to hear about what I'm doing with the forest sector national action plan. I mentioned that one of the key outputs was a toolkit for men as advocates on gender equality. They both were enthusiastically supportive and went on to tell me how they felt that more men would speak up if they had the right tools to do so. Clearly, there is a need to find the right approach, the right language, or perhaps, as I've said, develop EI skills. A toolkit can help ensure that the soil is fertile for communication of this kind.

Men as Advocates

Today, we are seeing a rapidly growing number of men who reject the old expectations of manhood and the notion of male superiority over women. There are more men willing to show immense respect for female co-workers and colleagues.

Men are also coming forward and vocalizing poor behaviour among men, including instances of hazing, which occurs in male-dominated sectors. Similarly, hockey players are coming forward and saying how they have been bullied. Harassment against men is now being brought into the open, shifting the conversation from a women's issue to an everyone's issue.

Men and women alike are rejecting traditional gender norms and recognizing that the human experience doesn't have to follow an either-or paradigm. LGBTQ rights are gaining ground, as are same-sex marriage rates. There is a growing societal acceptance of trans individuals. These are all signals of the start of an extraordinary and powerful shift toward gender diversity and inclusion. More and more men are agreeing with the goals of feminism, the equal right to an education, equal pay, and equal access to jobs. They too want an end to sexual harassment at work and violence against women in the home.

Kaufman shares, "In 1977 . . . 74 percent of US men thought that it's better for everyone if men earn the money while women take care of home and children. By 2008, just 30 years later, this had dropped to 40 percent." He continues, "Men are starting to challenge each other and challenge themselves. Men are speaking out in support of women's rights and marching in the streets, and men are embracing changes in what it means to be a man. And not only because it's good for the women they care about, but also because it's good for themselves. Change has happened, yes, but big challenges remain. Some of the biggest are in our workplaces."[62] As such, it is becoming increasingly evident that the macho man of yesterday is not the man of today or tomorrow.

A lot of men who were raised to be the macho men of yesterday now feel uncomfortable with that paradigm. In a sector-wide action plan that I spearheaded recently, one man expressed his discomfort with "the old boys' network." He shared a story about a client he'd had to wine and dine and had wanted to go to a "gentlemen's club." He stated he really didn't want to go. He had a wife at home who was pregnant and felt horrible about the idea of going, but he felt stuck. This was what the client wanted to do, so he went. He followed an old paradigm and pattern that is quickly becoming outdated. Fortunately, there's a space opening up now for men to start having this conversation. They weren't comfortable saying anything before because their objections would have been silenced in the culture of machismo and that hard construct of what masculinity is.

Let's return to how these concepts relate to corporate values. If the company for which this man worked valued respecting ones' boundaries, it would give him the backing to speak up and say he wasn't comfortable going there without fear of losing the client or corporate reprimand. Instead, it would allow employees to make a choice that fits within their own moral compass or comfort zone. This practice not only provides support to the employee, but it also allows for these types of interactions to advance to a new place, meaning the client may think twice before suggesting such a degrading activity the next time.

The author of a *Washington Post* article written after the 2017 explosion of the #MeToo movement, wrote that many women became annoyed or dismayed by the publicity attracted by the movement, believing that incidents of harassment in the workplace were common knowledge. But for the male writer, and presumably many other men, the pervasiveness of the problem came as quite a shock.[63]

In the 2016 Canadian General Social Survey (GSS), 19 percent of female respondents reported that they had experienced harassment in the workplace in the past year. In the survey harassment was defined as verbal abuse, humiliating behaviour, threats, physical violence, and/or unwanted sexual attention.[64] In other words, for roughly 1 in 5 women, this is old news. It is something that has always been there, that has always had to be navigated throughout the course of women's professional careers.

Yet, many wouldn't have spoken up before because they knew they wouldn't be supported. Perhaps they believed that it wasn't worth the trouble of speaking up, or they feared losing their jobs. Often people who speak up are perceived as troublemakers. Bosses don't want to deal with the unions, so they move her out instead of having a process in place to accurately seek the truth and hold people accountable for their behaviours.

To be clear, the shift that needs to happen isn't all on men. Women also have to set boundaries and speak up. If men overstep, women also have a role to play in providing clarity.

I had this kind of experience with a head-hunter in 2014. He made a comment about my looks and flat out suggested having sex with me. I replied saying, "If my light conversation and smiling on the margins of our professional relationship has given you the impression I am interested, I want you to know this is solely a professional relationship."

His face turned completely red and apologized. In an effort to move the relationship forward, I just said, "Let's put this behind us so we can continue our conversation."

Women must not dismiss these exchanges when we feel that the flirting has gone too far. It can only escalate to bigger flirtations that can be even harder to course correct.

An article published in 2019 by FSG, a consulting firm that addresses societal challenges, states that gender equity and equality cannot happen without engaging men and boys. It states, "Equity is relational. Inequities are rooted in uneven dynamics that give disproportionate power to one group versus another. Irrespective of the amount we invest in women, men also need to be willing participants in the redistribution of power between genders." The work in "increasing awareness of gender norms and empowering boys and men to feel confident in shifting their own behaviours is crucial to reaching greater equality."

The article also shares how companies can influence ingrained social norms by leveraging advocacy efforts and media campaigns. Some 30 years ago Gillette, a Procter & Gamble brand, aired an ad with the tagline, "the best a man can get." More recently, using the hashtag #TheBestMenCanBe, the company sparked a conversation on social and mass media regarding the stereotypes that men encounter that have a negative impact on women as well as on other men. The company complemented its advocacy efforts with a financial commitment to support organizations helping boys and men become positive role models. The old ad brought attention to the normalized, toxic masculinity that pervades society today, and through this campaign, Gillette not only called out harmful social norms but shed light on how addressing them supports gender equality and results in more positive outcomes for all. [65]

An Active Role to Play

As mentioned in chapter 1, the Women in the Workplace 2018 report demonstrated that women are underrepresented in the workplace at every level, especially in leadership positions. Although multiple factors contribute to that discrepancy, the passive role that men have historically played in supporting women's advancement is critical to the problem.[66]

FSG conducted research on gender inequality in the retail sector and found that career development opportunities are central to supporting women's advancement. For women in the workforce, particularly those early in their careers, having male advocates can significantly contribute to their career growth and success. I would argue, however, the early career support is easy—it's later on, when women are faced with the work-family balancing act, where men need to step it up.

Leveraging their influence and power, male leaders can not only support an individual woman's career but can also begin to create inclusive cultures that afford both men and women equal opportunities to advance.

Accountability for Behaviour

No one can argue that top executives have the power to change an organization. They can use this power and influence to set the values, put a boundary around those values to demonstrate they have meaning, and hold people accountable to those values.

It's important to have company values reinstated to the level of cultural tenets of the organization. Tying people's performance to the values of the organization is how to achieve real traction. By giving recognition to people who have demonstrated social intelligence skills that translate into greater team dynamics, leaders can help produce better business outcomes.

I believe having social intelligence as a corporate value will attract a diverse and inclusive workforce. It can start with the interview stage, asking questions that align performance against those skills. For example the interviewer can ask, "Tell me about a time when you asserted yourself and it led to a positive outcome." or "Tell me about a time when you were empathetic to a staff member."

An honest answer might be something like, "I never thought about that." But candidates might also recognize that, if they actually got into such a company, the support system and team they would be a part of on a day to day basis would be a game-changer.

Many people don't have that in their workplace, and it is the kind of corporate culture that men and women alike will want to go to. We want to work in a company that shares our own value sets. For many, that includes values around inclusivity, but everyone is attracted to being supported and being a part of great teams.

Leading companies today, such as Google, attest to having the greatest work environments and corporate cultures. However, the fact that they are facing sexual harassment lawsuits tells another story. Injecting some EI values into the heart of an organization could go a long way toward addressing lawsuit hiccups.

If we project what industry will look like in the next five or ten years, a lot of the workforce is going to be coming from around the world, bringing their own cultures and views on diversity and inclusion. There will be a need for organizations to have a corporate values statement on what is appropriate behaviour, according to clearly stated values, for men and women alike. That way, people aren't left blowing in the wind with a model that doesn't match the current work culture or hold any meaning.

Social intelligence can become a part of the corporate values of an organization. It can be a simple way for peers to help hold each other accountable, for supervisors to write accurate per-formance reviews, for HR professionals to conduct fair inves-tigations when things *don't* go well. Having this kind of frame-work for the company to use as a guidepost on behaviour and culture helps guide it toward superior in diversity and inclusion practices.

If an organization adopts inclusive values and says, "These are the values and behaviours that we are measuring, and they are core to our company," people from any walk of life can step in and know what is required of them and what they can expect from each other. Though at times they may have to check their personal belief systems at the door, clear expectations provide everyone with comfort in knowing that criticism, mockery, and backlash of any kind will not be tolerated.

The Results of Training in Social Intelligence Skills

By zeroing in on these skills for employees, the whole organization rises to a higher standard of respect in the workplace and a greater tolerance for differences. All of these qualities drive retention, innovative thinking, performance, and ultimately an increase to the bottom line.

Moreover, by evolving and harnessing our emotions, we are better to ourselves and all those around us. We become more tolerant of diversity and inclusion issues and more capable of managing people. We exhibit less resistance to change and are more open to new ideas.

Imagine a corporate culture with clearly defined boundaries built around strong company values. Corporate values today speak of things like collaboration, inclusiveness, and gender equality for all, but they can be expanded to include emotional intelligence skills.

If companies instill corporate value systems based on this new terminology and connect psychology to the corporate world, it can lead to massive positive transformation. It's about saying, "This is our tenet in our corporate structure. These are the values we ascribe to. If you come work for us, whether you are a male or a female, this is what we expect from you." Make this line in the sand and prepare to become a magnet for attracting top talent.

Takeaways

The statements below summarize the main points you can take away from this chapter.

- Diversity and inclusion is an everybody issue, not just a women's issue.
- Social intelligence is comprised of a suite of skills that should be written into the values in any company to create a culture that truly supports diversity and inclusion.
- By training social intelligence skills, companies see greater support for gender diversity and inclusion, leading to greater performance, innovation, creativity, and outcomes.

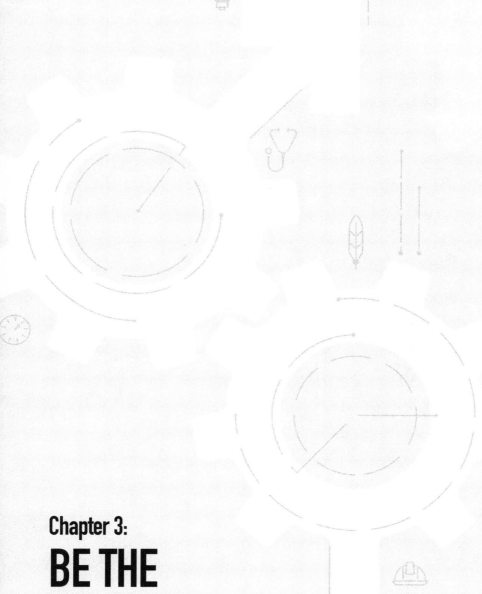

Chapter 3:
BE THE
CHANGE

One of the greatest leaders of the twentieth century, Mahatma Gandhi, is well known for the phrase, "You must *be* the change you want to see in the world." Being the change requires that you envision the desired future state and then emulate that in the present, while simultaneously guiding others to follow your lead. With gender equality in the workplace being that desired future state in this context, it is incumbent upon the leadership of the organization to demonstrate their commitment through their words and actions, set the new tone, and behave in a manner that supports the end goal.

Now that we know the business advantage of gender equality (chapter 1) and recognize the benefits of social intelligence skills to create the successful conditions for a respectful workplace (chapter 2), it is now necessary for us to figure out how to lead the charge.

Implementation can seem daunting at first. When broken down, however, and with all hands on deck, you will begin to see that it is a manageable shift and that you don't have to do it alone. I think part of the reason there is hesitation to do anything on GDI is because leaders don't have a clear path before them that they can implement. And without that certainty, the task can seem risky, meaning risk of failure, which no leader wants to have on his/her resume. But with a blueprint in hand, there is greater ability to take action.

Model and Commit

The first step toward leading the change is *being* the change your-self. Employees at all levels of the ladder will follow your example. If you articulate the business advantages, both verbally and in writing, of doing this and adhering to corporate values that support gen-der diversity and inclusion, it will become clear what behaviour is expected of them.

For some, this may require coaching. And that's okay. A lot of people find this topic to be full of pitfalls and murky waters. Some people don't know what to say anymore to women or how to conduct themselves. Coaching can help give guidance on what to say and what actions to take and can help foster an inclusive mindset.

A large-scale McKinsey study conducted in 2015 showed that when leaders modelled the behavioural changes they had asked their employees to make, the success rate jumped from 6 percent to 32 percent. This tells us something quite substantial; commit-ment is not optional.

Years of focus on gender diversity and inclusion across many industries have yielded one overwhelmingly consistent conclusion: The commitment of the most senior leader, such as the CEO or company President, is the critical ingredient.

For example, a Conference Board of Canada research study highlighted the difference between "passive" and "proactive" CEO support for gender diversity and inclusion. The conclusion was that only proactive support creates a successful outcome. Leaders, therefore, must be on the front lines in this shift.

The CEO alone cannot change the culture of the entire orga-nization. The executive team, the Human Resources team, and leaders throughout the company must also play their part. A recent McKinsey report concludes that in companies that suc-ceed with fostering gender-inclusive cultures and workplaces, the CEOs and senior executives "walk, talk, run, and shout about gender diversity and inclusion." They "fervently believe in the business benefits of creating an environment where talent can rise."

Champions show their commitment through constant communication and very visible actions. They ask questions, tell stories, and challenge assumptions. They get personally involved in key initiatives, and they consistently model inclusive behaviours.[67] From the top down, senior leaders and managers need to become champions of diversity and inclusion. As a leader in your organization, you are the hero in this story.

How to Take Action

You must make a formal commitment to employees and external audiences, stating that a concerted effort is taking place now to become a more inclusive company. Stating this intention holds the president and other senior leadership accountable, and accountability is the key to the success of a gender diversity and inclusion strategy. When employees have a manager who regularly challenges bias, as opposed to one who rarely does, they are more likely to think that everyone has an equal chance to advance at work.

All change must begin with senior leaders and managers. Not only are leaders responsible for the decisions that affect their employees' daily work experiences and overall career arc, but they also exemplify what's important to the company through their attitudes and priorities.

Consider these statistics from the Women in Mining Canada report:

- Only about one in three employees reports that senior leaders encourage an open dialogue on gender diversity or provides guidance on how to improve gender diversity.
- Just one in five employees believes that leaders are held accountable for results.

- Less than a third of employees say that managers often challenge biased language and behaviour when they see or hear it.
- Less than a third of companies share most gender diversity metrics with managers and leaders and offer financial rewards for making progress. Yet what gets measured and rewarded is typically what gets prioritized.
- Less than half of managers receive unconscious bias training, yet when they understand how bias impacts their decision-making, they make fairer, more objective decisions.

Lasting change can only be achieved when individuals in leadership positions are held accountable for integrating GDI practices into their decision-making to the same degree as any other essential business initiative. This requires training leaders so they truly understand this problem and how to solve it. They can make this commitment verbally, in writing, and by taking appropriate action.

Say It

There are different ways to vocalize and explain the commitment to gender diversity and inclusion in your organization and across the sector overall.

I'm spearheading a steering committee on gender equity for the forest sector national action plan project. The incredible individuals on the committee are all "saying it" by taking action with their own companies' policies and procedures and by participating in this sector-wide project. They are "being the change" by putting their voice behind the intent of the project. They are declaring to the world that their organizations see the benefits of gender diversity and inclusion, enough so to contribute their time and energy toward making it happen.

Say It in Your Own Company Policies and Procedures

Modernizing company language isn't sufficient by itself, but it's a necessary start. *How* company values are articulated says a lot about how seriously the company carries them out. This transition will involve looking at company policies, processes, or procedures already in place.

To encourage gender diversity and inclusion, look through your company's training and recruitment materials, vision and mission statements, and any other event, policy, or procedure manuals. Are there any areas, however subtle, that reflect barriers to women's full participation? For example, are job titles gender-inclusive? Can "foreman" be replaced with "team leader"? Can "manpower" be replaced with "staffing"? Keep in mind that many of your company's material, especially if you're in technical trades and science and engineering fields, were likely designed at a time before women held a significant presence in technical positions.

Consider how policies could be made more inclusive for women. Travel policies, for example, could reimburse taxi fares or the use of personal vehicles in recognition that some employees may feel unsafe taking public transit alone in certain locations or times of day.

Also ask yourself how your company's policies encourage work-life balance. Gender-inclusive companies look for ways to help employees fulfill the multiple roles in their lives. Implementing formal policies and the informal practices that support that balance has a direct impact on the bottom line. It has been proven that these endeavours result in reduced absenteeism, improved employee engagement, less stress, and improved health, to name just a few benefits.

Supporting employee work-life balance includes:

• A set of policies or programs to govern practices such as flex-time, working from home, personal leave, extended health benefits, Employee Assistance Program, practices to stay in touch with family while at remote work sites, taking or carrying over vacation days, managing overtime requirements, community childcare partnerships, and others

- Practices such as not having meetings that extend outside of core working hours and limiting email and other business contact outside of scheduled working hours
- Alignment of the informal and formal reward systems, including redefining the "ideal employee" for advancement to emphasize performance results over the number of hours worked

Review the company's performance management processes. Are there fair procedures in place for hiring and promotions? Are men and women equally offered regular opportunities for feedback and career advancement?

Training and mentoring can also support women in developing the skills needed to thrive in their positions. This is where EQ skills training comes in handy! Skill-building programs can be implemented to train women to work as heavy equipment operators or to become better public speakers. Training investments make good business sense, as there is usually a significant return on the investment.

There are cost-effective resources that can be tapped, such as training available through industry associations, women-focused agencies, and local colleges. One Women in Mining Canada offer successful resources, such as the following:

- An Edmonton-based organization, Women Building Futures, goes beyond just the hands-on work skills for construction or trades occupations. They focus on readiness-building, which includes intangible skills such as what to expect in camp life, how to adapt to shift work, and communication skills for various situations.
- Women in Resource Development Corporation, based in Newfoundland and Labrador, offers an Orientation to Trades

program, a database of mentors, and direct support to employers wanting to increase gender diversity.

- Aboriginal Women in Mining helps women prepare for the lifestyle changes required for working in mining. Women who were training for work in the Detour mine were required to leave home for a week, and this program supported them by addressing family issues and the personal impact of life at a remote worksite.

Take a look at the company's facilities and equipment. Are they appropriate for men *and* women? In sectors such as mining and forestry, field camps require different tenting arrangements, as well as work clothes in women's sizes. For example, Covergalls Workwear was recently launched and offer clothing designed for women working in the mining sector. Their designs allow women to go to the bathroom easily and ensure that they don't have dangerously long sleeves or pant legs, reducing the risk of oversized clothing getting caught in equipment.

Intentionally reviewing a company's culture and practices to uncover any remnants of the "old boys' club" paradigm is the first step toward relinquishing those age-old practices and removing systemic barriers to diversity and inclusion. This step allows companies the opportunity to:

- Provide training programs that build women's skills and readiness for positions where they are needed and traditionally under-represented.
- Design career paths that take account of career events that traditionally impact women such as parental, caregiving, or education leaves.
- Formalize and extend the benefits of networking by encouraging leaders and managers to mentor and advocate for talented women.
- Update talent management processes, such as definitions of potential and hiring and promotion criteria, to be gender inclusive.

- Be proactive about hiring and promoting by requiring efforts to ensure that short lists include qualified women for consideration.
- Probe further when HR firms tell you they can't find any women for a position. Job postings need to be reworded to focus on skillsets that are transferable, thereby attracting women from other sectors.

▷ Words Are Powerful

When terminology, images, facilities, and policies appear to be designed for men; it can make it more difficult to attract women into the industry.

These aren't matters of political correctness. They are subtle but powerful signals about the workforce and who is "in" and who is "out." In a competitive labour market, talented women will gravitate to workplaces that reach out to welcome them.

Those in high positions of leadership have a unique opportunity to be role models for others. They can lead the change to a new corporate social intelligence paradigm by calling out behaviours and decisions that are inconsistent with an inclusive culture. And they can become champions for flexibility and work-life balance, which will benefit men and women alike, as well as the bottom line.

Through research I've conducted for the forest sector national action plan, I've come across some useful actions for leaders to consider onboarding as they look for ways to make change happen in their organizations. Specifically, Elizabeth Broderick in the document "40:40:20 For gender balance: Interrupting bias in your talent processes" has shared relevant tips.[68]

▷ Actions for Leaders

- Personally engage in the development of job descriptions for your top team, defining future-focused requirements, including capabilities linked to potential.

- Challenge your team to rewrite job descriptions regularly and "deconstruct" requirements.
- Actively debunk traditional notions of "merit" by highlighting the diversity of skills and backgrounds of candidates or new hires and by celebrating the success of diverse teams.
- Demonstrate that you hire for potential and future capability requirements, not just experience, and ask the same of your teams.
- Recognize and reward those in your team who hire diverse talent and build diverse teams.
- Ask line managers what they have done to identify a pool of candidates that is gender-balanced, including where they have looked and who they have encouraged to apply.
- Ensure that the organization is tapping into diverse referrals and networks.
- Ensure that all jobs are advertised internally and externally to encourage a wide pool of candidates.
- Set clear expectations on gender-balanced shortlists before reviewing a shortlist to choose candidates to interview.
- Review your talent pipeline and personally review shortlists. Is the ratio of men to women fifty-fifty? If not, why?
- Participate in selection panels for key leadership appointments.
- Acknowledge and interrupt personal biases and call out behaviours and decisions that are inconsistent with building a diverse team.
- Make the decision to have gender-balanced panels, with external advisors, as appropriate.
- Mandate interview training and recruitment process compliance for your leadership team.
- Explore recruitment outcomes and their contribution to diversity objectives during routine performance discussions—use these discussions to help determine discretionary incentive payments.

- Personally champion gender pay parity and make transparent efforts to identify and close any gaps.
- When announcing appointments, highlight the diversity of skills, background, and experience all appointees bring to the team and organization.
- Hold line leaders accountable for achieving gender targets and include these as part of the key performance indicators (KPIs).
- Establish group scorecards that include gender targets to drive group-wide aspiration and achievement.
- Regularly review the last ten hires and the last ten employees who have left. Explore how bias has been effectively interrupted.
- Actively promote and celebrate the benefits of gender diversity—diverse leadership and diverse teams are central to improved performance.[69]

Paying attention to these actions is key to successful implementation. Most likely, you will need to hire someone full-time to manage a successful shift in the culture, which I'll further discuss later in this chapter.

The bottom line is, as a senior executive, you have to set the tone for the company. What you say and do is critical to its success. Everyone is paying close attention.

Say It at the Sector Level

Other ways to take a leadership role on gender diversity and inclusion is to either spearhead a sector-wide initiative in your industry or participate in one that is already up and running.

Beyond the mining and forest sector national action plans on gender diversity that I've led and told you about, there are declarations being made in other sectors. Canada's energy sector, for example, has engaged C-suites to formally declare that they will commit to a diversity accord. The "Leadership Accord on Gender

Diversity" is a public commitment by Canadian employers, educators, unions, and governments to promote the values of diversity and inclusion within their organizations. Participants sign a certificate of commitment and declaration, which sets into motion the implementation of initiatives that support their commitment to diversity. Advocates engage in outreach, promotion, and communication with constituencies, while encouraging them to sign similar declarations. Two years after signing, a gender gap audit is conducted on the organization's progress and gives feedback to those responsible for implementing the change.[70]

An article by McKinsey and Company (2015) titled "A CEO's Guide to Gender Equality" speaks to the importance of getting CEOs to make formal commitments to diversity and inclusion and states that "change initiatives must be a strategic priority to have any chance of success." The study results noted a 5.3x increase in performance when leaders role-modelled the behaviours they expected their employees to make.

One initiative by the Mining Industry Human Resources (MIHR) Council is a great example of a formal, explicit commitment to GDI. The MIHR's Gender Champions Taskforce piloted a "Being a Gender Champion" executive workshop to train senior leaders to be gender champions by advocating for gender-inclusive workplaces and working toward change at the organization *and* sector levels.

▷ Strategic Executive Reflection

The McKinsey study also found that companies that make progress tend to hold a series of challenging conversations about gender issues among their executive teams. Bringing in a gender expert to coach the executive through a strategic, reflective discussion can help get everyone on the same page and rowing in the same direction. It can also be an opportunity to share biases and belief systems that, once aired, allow for new learning among the group and a stronger united path forward.

Drawing from some initial thinking from the "Male Champions of Change" organization, I suggest a strategic session that covers questions such as the following:

- How transparent am I about my own practices to manage my own work-life balance?
- How comfortable am I with addressing my own biases? What are they?
- What signal does the gender composition of my top team send to my organization?
- How effectively am I sponsoring women to ensure equal access to opportunities?
- Does my team exemplify how to blend different views and ways of operating?
- How do I reward and promote people with a track record of inclusive leadership?
- If men dominate my team, how do I acknowledge the imbalance and take visible steps to remedy it?
- How do I create gender balance when selecting people to lead major initiatives?
- How clear are standards of acceptable and desired behaviours? How consistent are the consequences when standards are not met?
- How would my team describe our gender balance expectations and level of priority?
- How transparent is my team about the selection criteria for senior roles?
- How much time do I spend with senior and emerging women leaders? How well do I understand their perspectives and priorities?
- How do I ensure that our systems and processes enable flexibility?

Many company leaders have asked these questions when embarking on GDI strategies and have integrated their executive team thinking into next steps. The answers help provide clarity on how to become a positive example of a gender-inclusive workplace.

Show It

Showing your commitment to gender diversity and inclusion begins with checking how ready your organization really is for this change initiative. Develop your business case and create focus group conversations that are two-way communications, for senior leadership to explain what is going to happen and employees to give feedback on what is happening at their level.

Develop a Readiness Assessment

Demonstrating your commitment to action on gender diversity and inclusion starts with conducting a pre-assessment to get a sense of the organization's readiness for the change. Conducting a quick survey with employees to get a pulse on their ability to absorb a culture change is a helpful first step and one that is often underestimated and overlooked. The following list of questions can help guide this assessment:

- Are there change initiatives currently underway?
- Have previously implemented change initiatives been successful, or did they fail?
  ◇ Was executive support for the change weak or strong?
- Is this company top-down driven? Or are all employees made to be empowered?
- Do people take accountability for their actions?
- Do you expect your organization to be hesitant to or accepting of a GDI culture shift?
  ◇ Do you anticipate pockets of resistance from some employee groups or strong resistance from certain managers?
  ◇ How has your organization dealt with resistance to culture changes in the past?

Answers to questions such as the ones noted above help you gauge your audience. It enables you to gain a quick lay of the land for the receptivity of what you're about to embark on.

As an additional tip, one potential pitfall to keep in mind is "change fatigue." If other change initiatives are currently underway, and if there is constant change occurring, it can feel exhausting. Be empathetic to employees in this regard and explain that you recognize the challenge. It will go a long way toward getting them engaged from the get-go.

Develop Your Own Business Case

In order to take actionable steps, not only does a formal commitment need to be made, but the proper allocation of resources needs to be given, both financial and human, toward implementing the change.

Typically, it's the C-suite who makes these kinds of decisions, so those who already see the need and have the desire to implement diversity and inclusion in the company need to present their case to the decision-makers in charge. Outline the reasons you want to invest resources toward this effort and use your own company's numbers to demonstrate the return on investment.

When making your case, explain that one of the first steps is to appoint a gender diversity and inclusion (GDI) officer, someone who reports directly to the president and is accountable for the successful execution of the GDI strategy.

Hire a GDI Officer

Outline the reasons why you want to hire a GDI officer. For instance, describe the commitments their role will undertake, such as:

- Increasing the recruitment of women, regardless of race or religion

- Engaging with more women-owned businesses as part of the supply chain
- Ensuring equitable consultation and engagement with male and female community members, should your projects impact a community

Provide context for the position. Will the officer have a team and an office? Who will they report to? Has their work program already been clearly defined?

The GDI officer is the company's lead on gender diversity and equity initiatives. Their role is to develop a business case for gender equity by identifying key drivers for improving diversity within the company, such as the value proposition noted in chapter 1. They will then consolidate these drivers into a company-specific business case, outlining ways that these improvements will create business benefits.

The GDI officer's responsibilities will include:

- Gaining buy-in from senior management and other key players in support of gender diversity and inclusion messaging
- Working with HR, procurement, communications, and community engagement to develop diversity action plans and programs, including identifying independent teams to conduct a gender audit and pay gap study where required
- Providing organization-wide coordination of diversity efforts
- Assisting with external and internal messaging of the company's diversity commitments

While certain in-house staff might qualify for the role of your organization's gender equity champion, be sure that they have the necessary time to do the job. Too many times employers add the role to an employee's existing full-time responsibilities (usually the highest-ranking female), which is not sustainable or effective. At minimum, the GDI Officer's job should be considered a half-time position, although my recommendation is to designate it as a full-time position.

When stating your case, it will help to link the GDI strategy to the company's overall strategy. Tie in the company's brand, culture, and values with the direction the company can take by realizing the GDI strategy.

Sodexo, featured in a case study in chapter 1, is an example of a company that has done an excellent job of creating its own company values and using those values to develop an overall business and brand strategy, thereby achieving a unique competitive advantage.

In addition to demonstrating the financial incentives to GDI, there are everyday actions that leaders can take to show their commitment to creating a safe and respectful work environment. After all, how we lead, through action or inaction, sets the tone for everyone else in the company.

Hold Focus Group Discussions

One of the helpful things you can do as the leader for a change initiative is to hold a few focus group meetings with the executive, middle managers, and employees in a series of roundtable discussions to help them understand first-hand what you're intending to roll out across the company and to be visibly and actively setting the tone for what's to come.

I've seen this done effectively before on mental health issues when I worked in the federal government. A senior executive took the time to meet with various levels of his department and share what efforts were underway to support those with mental health issues. It was also a venue to hear from employees about issues in the workplace that were creating mental health problems. Similarly, executives can hold focus group discussions with women *and* men to discuss what is going to happen in the organization to create gender equality and provide them with a space for feedback on the conditions people are working in. This open and transparent approach to communication establishes a level of credibility for the leaders, as they are showing they are interested and committed enough to take the time to hear what is important to employees.

The following are some action items for leaders to utilize in focus group discussions. A report by Male Champions for Change provides excellent examples of ways leaders can show their commitment to gender-inclusive cultures.[71]

▷ *Respond to 'jokes'*

- *Do not validate humor that is explicitly or implicitly sexist or offensive by laughing, staying silent, or making excuses.*
- *Call out the joke, for example, say: "What did you mean by that comment?"*
- *If you miss the moment to call it out, don't let it pass - ensure both the joker and those who heard it are aware of your stance.*

▷ *Value women's voices*

- *Ensure equal share of voice at meetings you lead or attend.*
- *Before closing a meeting or agenda item, ensure everyone has been provided the opportunity to comment or contribute*
- *Ensure all contributions/contributors to a discussion or initiative are acknowledged – beyond the most senior and/or vocal.*
- *Adopt the Panel Pledge to ensure high profile discussions and forums include the voices and experiences of women.*

▷ *Make role stereotyping a thing of the past*

- *Ensure critical and ancillary roles at functions, meetings and in your workplace are shared equally amongst men and women, for example rotate meeting note taker and chair.*
- *Question assumptions about the type of work, especially physical, that men and women can and cannot do.*

▷ *Keep the focus on capability, not appearance*

- *Keep conversations focused on content and capabilities, rather than physical appearance.*
- *Be vigilant when introducing women for example, as speakers or at meetings where comments about appearance can undermine credibility.*

▷ *Support personal choices about caring and careers*

- *Check whether you are making assumptions about, or choices for women or men regarding how they value or prioritize their career.*
- *Ensure equal access to flexible work arrangements for women and men within your organization.*

▷ *Challenge gender labelling*

- *Recognize where gender stereotypes are being applied to assess performance or leadership capability.*
- *Reframe a discussion anytime an employee or candidate is assessed as 'too' anything – 'too bossy,' 'too soft,' 'too emotional,' etc.*

Some of these tips above may seem obvious, like "keep the focus on capability, not appearance," and I agree. That should be obvious. But I have seen many times when both men and women have highlighted how a woman appears: what she's wearing, or her physique. Unfortunately, I have experienced for myself what it feels like to be judged based on appearance.

When I was in my mid-thirties, I was asked to speak to an audience of roughly 100 people about a project I was leading in the federal government. My boss introduced me and started with, "I'd like to introduce the very capable and svelte Kelly Cooper..." I thought *Did I just hear what I think I just heard? Really?*

I was completely embarrassed by his comment and had to get up to the podium trying to pretend I hadn't heard it and blocking out the thought that those in the audience were without doubt judging me according to my appearance instead of listening to what I had to say. Plus, I was already a bit nervous about speaking to a large audience, so this only added to that feeling. It was a clueless move on my boss's part, and to this day, I still can't believe it happened.

Conversations in small groups that highlight these kinds of behaviours provide an opportunity for people to ask questions and fully understand the direction being taken. They help create ambassadors/champions in your organization, who encourage the kinds of behaviours you are aiming for.

Checklist for Showing Commitment to Gender Diversity & Inclusion [72]

- Make a statement to all staff, in person and in writing, about the importance of gender diversity.
  - ◇ Explain the business case and how the strategy is in alignment with corporate priorities. The GDI Officer could take the lead in this effort.
- Appoint a senior executive leader for gender diversity and inclusion.
  - ◇ The senior point person can be male or female but should have time allocated specifically for this role.
- Explain all company measures to be taken to support GDI in the workplace.
  - ◇ Ensure that staff understand the reasons it is a corporate priority and that the efforts are part of a plan for a more productive and successful business model, rather than a plan to prioritize women over men.
- Communicate the corporate position on gender diversity and inclusion and the measures in place to achieve it within corporate reporting so that stakeholders are aware of the company's position and efforts.

- Take a prominent and transparent role in addressing gender diversity and inclusion complaints or concerns across the company.
- Publicly encourage implementation of GDI policies.
  ◇ Take the lead in driving the development and adoption of policies such as equal-pay-for-equal-work, flex-work policies, and maternity and paternity care.
- Foster a work environment that encourages staff to access GDI policies without jeopardizing their growth in the company.
- Develop and support incentive programs for gender diversity and inclusion, such as financial incentives and awards for teams that meet gender diversity and work-life balance goals.

This chapter was meant to give you guidance on how to get started and take action. Remember, this GDI strategy starts with you. Just like in sports, the better the coach, the better the team.

When you hold yourself accountable for seeing these new policies and procedures through and allocating the necessary resources to be able to take action, the rest of the team will follow.

 Takeaways

The statements below summarize the main points you can take away from this chapter.

- Participate in events that allow leaders across your sector to share knowledge and discuss progress on gender advancement within their companies.
- There are many actions you can take right away to get things started. If you don't know what to do, take time with a gender expert coach to position yourself to move forward.
- Be visible and take action often. Be a challenger within your executive team when it comes to their words and actions.
- Stay engaged.

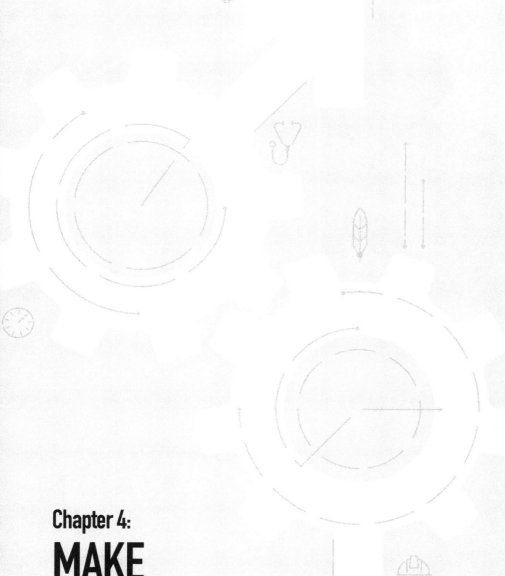

Chapter 4:
MAKE
THE CHANGE

"Make it happen." is something we often hear from bosses that just want to see the job done. When making a gender diversity and inclusion strategy and a culture shift that allows women and other minorities to be a greater part of the workforce composition of the company, "Make it happen." is a tall order.

As I shared with you earlier, when I was tasked with implementing a large IT change initiative across eight federal departments, I was told to go home and write up the strategy and have it done in one day. It was crazy talk.

Anyone who knows anything about affecting culture change knows that it is not something that one individual can or should attempt to do by themselves. I felt not only that my boss was missing the mark on what needed to happen, but that I was being set up for failure. Why? Because it requires overcoming people's views, beliefs, mindsets, and emotional triggers. In short, it requires the engagement of everyone to learn new skills and new knowledge in a safe and trusting environment. If done properly, it can happen in a systematic way, allowing people to engage step-by-step and easing them into the transition by way of clear, simple, and gradual changes.

This chapter is focused on how to go about implementing a GDI strategy in the most logical and succinct manner I can deliver. I don't get into all the nitty-gritty details here, and that's intentional.

There are too many nuances within each individual organization. It's best to give the overarching path, and when you're ready to engage a GDI expert, you can delve into your own particular context and zero in on the aspects that are most relevant to your particular work environment.

To successfully shift a workplace culture from male-dominated to inclusive of all genders and cultures, it's key to recognize that the secret sauce is how you *engage and communicate* with people. There will be resistance from some. Others will quickly adopt the process. And a whole lot of folks will be fence-sitters, waiting to see if this is just the latest fad, or if it will be around for the long haul.

To simplify things right off the bat, a GDI strategy needs to be broken down into three main phases: Planning, Design, and Implementation.

Phase 1: Planning

Now that the case for hiring a gender diversity and inclusion officer has been made and that individual has been identified, steps must be taken to set that person and the organization up for success. Although the importance of having leadership on board and acting as a role model/sponsor has already been emphasized, I must stress that leaders cannot simply act in silos when implementing a strategy for gender diversity and inclusion across the organization. They need the support of a team to make the change.

Form a GDI Task Force

The first step the GDI officer should take to establish a diverse and inclusive company is to form a GDI task force. The task force should ensure representation from all departments across the company. (Note: Don't shy away from including naysayers. They often become the strongest advocates once they understand the benefits!)

To demonstrate the principles of diversity and inclusion, the task force itself should include people with a variety of backgrounds. Fresh insights will come from a blend of operations and administrative functions; women and men, new hires and long-term employees, parents and single people, and people of different generations and cultures. People with new perspectives will be able to challenge the status quo and question myths and misconceptions about women and men in the workplace.[73]

The team should include members from human resources, communications, marketing, and representatives from every business unit and job grade organization wide. If this seems totally unrealistic, you'll have to find a way to get key people on the task force that can move through many different circles of influence.

When developing the gender champions committee for the forest sector national action plan project, I had to be strategic about who would sit on the committee. There was a lot of interest from many parts of the sector, for example many industry representatives came forward. But we had to consider representation across the country and across the sector. I set up criteria for who would sit on the committee so we could have a critical review of who should participate. This also served as a means of justifying who was chosen, in the event that anyone questioned how people were selected. Part of the criteria for selection was how each individual could influence and reach others. I also had a criteria to get as close as possible to a fifty-fifty representation of male to female participants.

Each representative on the task force will come to the table with their own perspective on whether or not gender diversity and inclusion is needed for the business or not. As such, one of the first things the task force must do is get on the same page. That means ensuring that all comments and views are aired.

People must have the time to understand the business case, contribute to the end goal, and develop a sense of trust that the initiative required for success. People will then feel empowered with knowledge and secure in knowing that their time is being spent on something that will make a difference. Plus, task force members need to feel confident that the shift will happen so that they can safely ask those they intend to influence to trust them.

The role of the task force is to:

1. Set goals and targets for a gender diversity and inclusion strategy
2. Outline the strategy
3. Manage monitoring and accountability for those targets
4. Update senior management on progress while identifying and garnering support for necessary course corrections

As the leader of the task force, the GDI officer's duties will include:

Managing task force meetings, including drafting clear agendas, recording notes, and sharing them to be approved by the task force

1. Leading the development of gender diversity and inclusion targets
2. Monitoring, documenting, and evaluating progress toward targets and sharing that information with the communications team (so they can update employees, management, and stakeholders)
3. Acting as the point person for all contracts (gender audit, pay gap reviews, etc.)
4. Reporting directly to the president on the strategy

Set Company-wide Goals and Targets for GDI

Once a task force is created, it's time to establish "targets with teeth." That means specific, ambitious goals that are aligned with your company wide GDI strategy.

One study found that specific GDI targets lead to substantial overall progress in GDI initiatives, while a lack of targets will actually cause companies to *lose* ground.[74] In other words, the failure to set appropriate and specific targets will hamstring your GDI strategy right out of the gate.

One important note to keep in mind: Targets should *not* be focused on goals dictating the number of women in the workplace. Goals that are perceived as quotas will create unnecessary concerns and risk a narrow, short-term focus. Rather, targets can and should include measures around new ways of working together. For example:

- More respectful interactions
- Inclusive meeting practices (e.g., how the chair of a meeting ensures equal airtime)
- Flexibility in where and when some of the work gets done (e.g., not scheduling meetings to end after 5 p.m.)

Targets can also assess indicators that are positive for everyone, like less absenteeism, reduced turnover, and greater satisfaction measures on employee surveys. Numbers are just one of many possible indicators of progress.

It's also worth noting that a company's goals will vary depending on the their stage of development. A company that is just taking its first step toward GDI may have very different goals from an organization that has already taken some steps and is aiming to continue the journey. It's good to be ambitious, but you can't put the cart before the horse. You'll have to cultivate a respectful workplace culture to reduce your turnover before you can hope to leverage the innovation that goes hand in hand with gender-diverse leadership.

Tolko Industries Ltd., a privately owned forest company based in British Columbia, recently published a letter from the president about their focus on building a strong culture through company values. It was the main message in their February 2020 newsletter to all stakeholders and is a great example of how to show leadership straight from the top when leading a culture shift.

For those who may be questioning the impact a letter like that makes, let me assure you, it makes a big difference. The president is using his or her words and actions to illustrate the kind of culture he or she wants to have in the company. Holding people accountable to that standard is the follow-through that will be needed. But if everyone knows what the president expects, everyone will be able to reference his or her words to hold each other accountable. Plus, it gives employees comfort to know that senior management is putting a firm boundary around respect in the workplace and won't tolerate anything less.

To achieve a culture that supports greater gender diversity and inclusion, companies could start with a wide focus, such as fostering a respectful workplace, or a narrower one, such as hiring more women as heavy equipment operators.

Another successful approach is to focus on small wins, "a series of controllable opportunities of modest size that produce visible results by building a pattern that attracts allies and minimizes resistance." Years of applied research in a range of organizations has shown that a disciplined small-wins strategy for gender diversity and inclusion "benefits not just women but also men and the organization as a whole."[75]

Whatever the approach, take a long-term perspective on GDI actions rather than settling for a quick fix. Knowing the current state of your organization will help identify the opportunities and the likely challenges in becoming more inclusive of women.

Benchmarking indicators of the current state might be readily available on hiring, promotions, turnover rates, records of complaints or grievances, engagement survey results, absenteeism and wellness indices, and others. Additional indicators of a workplace culture could be gathered through interviews or observations on expectations of work-life balance, interactions in meetings, respectful behaviours, etc.

Your assessments will identify natural strengths, areas of weakness, and opportunities for achieving tangible business benefits and early wins; and the information will help to shape an appropriate strategy with a high likelihood of success.

The GDI growth continuum chart below serves as a gauge to track progress over time.[76]

TABLE 1:
GENDER DIVERSITY & INCLUSION GROWTH CURVE

6 Lead the way

5 Integrate

4 Realize

3 Adapt

2 Begin

1 Comply

STAGE ON THE CONTINUUM
CHARACTERISTICS

1 COMPLIERS (At present)

· These companies (or industries) tend to do only what is required to comply with employment equity/human rights legislation.

[9] Adapted from the continuum proposed by MacBride-King & McLean (2006).

2 BEGINNERS (At present)

· Willing to do more than the minimum.
· Tend to focus on "fixing" their numbers and representation rates.
· Often have programs focused on resolving gender 'problems' such as conflicts, harassment or bullying.

3 ADAPTERS (At present)

· Have moved beyond a focus on employment equity and representation numbers.
· Often experiment with several programs/initiatives/policies.
· Realize that subtle barriers might exist; lack a coordinated approach.
· Diversity is seen primarily as an HR responsibility.

4 REALIZERS (At present)

· Understand the importance of diversity for business success.
· Vision/mission/values highlight the importance of diversity.
· Show early movement toward an integrated approach to gender diversity and inclusion; a few strategic initiatives are successfully under way.
· Leaders throughout the organization champion diversity, and the organization invests in it.

5 INTEGRATORS (At present)

· Taking an integrated approach to diversity.
· Gender diversity and inclusion is embedded in the culture
· Internal accountability. frameworks are established
· Supplier and partner diversity initiatives are established and aligned.

6 COMMUNITY LEADERS

· Engaged in community-wide efforts to educate/inform others about diversity.
· Active proponents of community-wide efforts.
· Role models of diversity and inclusion.

It helps to make a list of the task force's goals, arranged in order of priority. Then identify key gender diversity targets for each priority goal and draft targets that align with key corporate goals. After the task force has identified the goals and targets for GDI, the GDI Officer should discuss and validate them with senior management. Every team member needs to understand, support, and buy in to those goals.

Phase 2: Design

The design phase is essentially putting a master plan in place that includes many key components, from developing a business plan straight through to developing a performance measurement plan. It will involve the collective input from the task force team with the GDI officer taking the lead on writing it and, of course, regular check-ins with the lead sponsor or senior executive. Having a gender expert involved in this phase is helpful in guiding the GDI officer on managing the task force and developing the strategy.

Hold an initial meeting with the task force to air views on GDI and create alignment on attitudes, beliefs, goals, and expectations for this initiative. This way, the task force will be able to hit the ground running.

Develop a GDI Strategy

Based on the key goals and targets identified, outline a strategy that effectively states how the company will achieve these goals, by whom, and when. The strategy should be a simple, straightforward document that includes the following sections:

- *Introduction/context:* This section should outline the key goals and objectives, the business case, including a summary of diagnostics and the company's current status on meeting these goals, as well as a change readiness analysis and anticipated areas of resistance.[77] As with any business plan, it should outline resources to be allotted (human and financial) and a SWOT analysis for this change at this time.

- **Communications plan:** This plan is critical, as it needs to include all stakeholders and specific tactics for each target audience. For example, how you communicate with people at head office about this initiative will be different from how you communicate with people working in the field.

- **Leader / Sponsor Actions:** The sponsor or leader of the GDI strategy has a key role. Understanding what that is will be key to a successful strategy (see Leader/Sponsor Actions graph on page 135). Consider this a leadership strategy that provides clarity on exactly what is expected of senior management to successfully implement GDI across their organization.

- **Resistance plan:** This section outlines how you will get ahead of those naysayers and prepare leaders for tough conversations.

- **Policies and program development:** Review current policies to see how they are worded, what they address now, and whether they incorporate the thinking of the end state of the GDI strategy. Develop specific programs that create the right course-corrections in upward mobility for gender-diverse and inclusive employees.

- **Plans for training and skills development:** Whether it's the implementing social intelligence skills training or increasing cultural awareness communications, include your plan to invest in skills development.

- **Roles and responsibilities:** Outline who is leading which component. Identify resources (financial as well as human) required to execute the specific action.

- **Performance measurement strategy:** Define how and when progress will be monitored and reported, as well as when the plan will be reviewed, revised, and updated to support continued progress. Also, identify targets to be achieved and define a process for gathering baseline data to begin tracking performance progress.

- **Recognition:** Create a summary of incentives and rewards and what a recognition program will look like.

Once these components are agreed upon by the task force, have each member share the strategy with their specific business units so that all teams understand their responsibilities, accountability, and opportunities for input and revision. This activity will familiarize everyone with the strategy and reinforce corporate objectives and commitments, as well as the role each business unit is expected to play.

Identify Outcomes and Enablers

It's important to remember that this GDI strategy is a process, and the *psychology of the change* is at the heart of the culture shift. It takes time and is as much about the journey as it is about the destination.

The GDI strategy is designed to achieve specific outcomes for the business.

By setting clear outcomes, you can track and measure progress toward the end goal of a GDI culture. Table 2 provides main outcomes to be achieved with corresponding actions that can be implemented to achieve them. This list is by no means exhaustive but gives you some ideas to get started.

Phase 3: Implementation

All key business units should be represented across the organization on the task force. It should include naysayers and supporters alike. Once assembled, all members need to be in alignment on the vision. Use a gender strategist to facilitate a consensus-building discussion if need be. Then define who is doing what and how, and you'll be in a great position to execute the actions in the strategy.

TABLE 2:
GDI OUTCOMES

Outcomes	Enablers
Awareness of the need to have an increase in gender diversity and inclusion	- Ready access to information - Stakeholder inputs - Marketplace changes - political drivers? - Management communications
Improved interest to participate and support a GDI strategy	- Disconnect with current state - Imminent negative consequences - Enhanced job security - Affiliation and sense of belonging - Career advancement - Incentive or compensation - Trust and respect for leadership - Hope in future state
Knowledge acquired on how to do this (empowers staff and help them feel a part of the process)	- Training and education - Information access - examples and case studies
Ability to implement the required skills and behaviours	- Practice applying new skills or using new processes and tools - Coaching - Mentoring
Reinforcement to sustain gender diversity and inclusion	- Incentives and rewards - Compensation changes - Celebrations - Personal recognition

As much as I enjoy the challenge of convincing people that a GDI strategy is key to business success, I also love getting into implementing the strategy. This phase is where you start putting words into actions, and with actions come results. That fires me up.

Actions are where the rubber meets the road, where the fence-sitters start perking up and paying closer attention because things are happening and results are starting to roll in. You can generate excitement with results, both social and financial, and then you build momentum that has an incredible impact progress.

I've found this with sector strategies. Initially, it required a lot of heavy lifting on my part to get the task force built and get everyone on the same page quickly. But the momentum that was built as a result was just amazing to watch. I measure momentum by the willingness of task force members to contribute their time and stay engaged in what we're doing.

It's been amazing. In the first year of the forest sector national action plan, I saw in-kind contributions from all members that matched the dollar value of the project. That tells me people saw the merit in what we were doing and wanted to help make a difference.

In the Phase 2: Design section, I identified many of the things that are needed in a GDI strategy. The majority of these steps can be understood based on their titles, but a couple may not be quite as clear, namely the Leader / Sponsor Actions and the Resistance Plan, so I'm going to focus on explaining what those two things are. If there are other parts of the strategy that aren't clear to you, a gender expert can help clarify them for you and put them in context according to your own needs.

Leader / Sponsor Actions

I find a leader/sponsor actions map to be an excellent tool to clarify the role leaders need to play to shepherd a GDI strategy from vision to action. The leader/sponsor in this context means the person who is leading the initiative. It is often the president but can also be the GDI officer who has regular access to the president. Specifically, the leader/sponsor actions map identifies the key activities and responsibilities needed to support the GDI strategy.

TABLE 3:
LEADER / SPONSOR ACTIONS

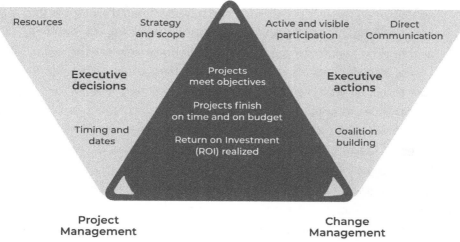

'Best Practices In Change Management', 2014 edition, Prosci benchmarking report.

Leaders/sponsors, as mentioned in chapter 3: Be the Change, should build awareness through articulating their vision, set the tone for what is to come, and be visible throughout implementation, ensuring it is being guided through to fruition.

The GDI task force is responsible for developing the leader/sponsor actions, outlining the activities the sponsor must perform to manage the GDI strategy. There are certain actions the sponsor needs to take at different phases of implementation. The diagram above lays out sponsor activities.

On the project management side, the leader/sponsor has a decision-making role in terms of how many resources will be provided, the timeline for implementation, and the scope for the project. (For example, will this project be comprised of one business unit? One office location? Or across the whole company?)

In terms of the people side of things, the executive sponsor has a role in direct communication with employees, coalition-building with peers and managers, and active and visible participation throughout the entire project.

When it comes to sector-wide plans, I've been there. I have personally been the leader/sponsor and have handled the responsibilities of identifying and finding the resources, setting the timeline, and finding task force members to collaboratively set the vision. I have also done many things to build a tight coalition across the task force, be visible across the sector by making presentations at conferences to engage a larger audience, and provide direct communication with task force members and anyone in the sector interested in learning more. Sometimes even members of the media have sought information about sector activity from me.

Although this process requires a lot of effort, especially at the front end, I find that using a leader/sponsor actions map works very effectively. And if you take what I've done on a sector-wide basis and adapt it into a company or organization perspective, you'll find that the same approach applies.

Through the active involvement of the leader/sponsor on both the project management and people side of implementing the GDI strategy, the middle triangle of items can be tracked. Measurement ensures that the GDI strategy is meeting its objectives—finishing on time and on budget—and that there is a measurable return on investment.

▷ Return on Investment

ROI is always the tricky part for people to understand. Costs will be put toward, making the strategy real throughout the organization, but financial results won't be seen for some time.

Leading companies that have made it through this process successfully will tell you that it takes anywhere from three to five years to see results, but keep in mind that you will see wins sooner at certain milestones.

Three to five years may seem like a long time, but when you think about the fundamental shift you're making, it's really not. We have been in a male-dominated culture since time immemorial; surely, we can manage to see that five years or less is well worth our time to move our corporate culture to the next level of how to operate in the workplace. While economic benefits may not be seen during the first year, you will be able to witness social improvements, such as well-being in the office environment and less turnover of staff, much more quickly.

▷ The Critical Role of the Leader/Sponsor

The leader/sponsor activities align nicely into the three phases of the project, Planning, Design, and Implementation. There are many actions for the sponsor to do in each phase, and I highly recommend a conversation with a gender expert to help guide the sponsor through what their particular situation is and what they're aiming to do.

For example, the Planning phase includes things like selecting the right GDI officer as the lead, identifying resources, and setting priorities for the work. If the leader/sponsor does project work themselves, they prevent task force members from fully participating. The Design phase includes duties such as attending key project meetings, holding the task force accountable for results, and being accessible to the GDI officer and task force when necessary. Lastly, the Implementation phase includes actions such as removing a roadblock, helping overcome obstacles, resolving conflict issues, and responding to any escalation that may arise.

Suffice it to say that with each phase, the leader/sponsor plays a key role in the success of the GDI strategy. There are also ways to help coach the leader/sponsor throughout the process, and I highly recommend it. Coaching the sponsor, first and foremost, helps establish a foundation for the right language, mindset, and understanding from which to springboard into the various audiences in the company who will be listening carefully to what is being said and done by the lead on this initiative.

Developing a Resistance Strategy

Gene Rodenberry, the creator of *Star Trek*, understood diversity and inclusion back in 1964 when he had his senior crew members of the *Enterprise*, comprised of a mix of cultures from around the galaxy. We watched this futuristic world with great interest and never thought anything of it. Lieutenant Uhura, a Black female, was the head of communications, and Commander Sulu, portrayed by an Asian American actor, was chief engineer. Later iterations of the show, with Jean-Luc Picard at the helm, continued the practice of representing diversity and inclusion with the chief medical officer being a woman and a Black man, Worf, as the command division bridge officer, among other notable characters. Viewers seemed to buy in to this basic premise of diversity and inclusion, as evidenced by the many years the show carried on.

One famous episode of *Star Trek: The Next Generation* captured the idea of the collective thinking with the Borg. The Borg were a monolithic alien entity that represented the collective wisdom and thoughts of a culture that dominated all others. When one came across the Borg, they were quickly assimilated. The Borg's mantra was "Resistance is futile." However, there was one resistor. In the episode "I, Borg," an adolescent Borg named Hugh. Hugh, unlike the rest of the Borg, refused to be assimilated.

Let me be clear—I am not implying that the issue of GDI is the same as the Borg, but it is a wave of change that is coming through the workplace, and, given the multicultural world we live in, it's not going away.

It's important to recognize there will always be a Hugh in any corporate culture shift—someone who will resist the change. It's naive to think everyone will be on board. However, it's also important to find ways to communicate and engage with those individuals. Rather than taking a hard-line, resistance-is-futile approach, education is often the secret weapon.

Resistance is the natural reaction to change. People are creatures of habit, and they enjoy the comfort and stability that comes with it. Moreover, every individual has a threshold of how much change they can absorb based on their personal history, current events in their lives, and current changes at work. Even when employees align the change with their self-interests and belief systems, the uncertainty of success and fear of the unknown remain significant barriers to change.

A resistance strategy should be included in the overall GDI strategy. This is a matter of (a) being proactive in addressing concerns, and (b) building acceptance and commitment in your employees to pave the way toward the desired result.

It's helpful to note that those who benefit the most from the status quo will be the ones most likely to resist change. Don't be discouraged. In many cases, increased resistance from these individuals indicates that you're moving in the right direction.

Below is a table of the most common forms of resistance.[78] Chances are, you've experienced at least one of these before, though I suspect you've experienced many of them at one time or another.

Some of these ideas in the following chart are taken from the report by VicHealth (2018) "(En)countering resistance: Strategies to respond to resistance to gender equality initiatives." However, I have added additional thinking on other forms of resistance that stem from women in particular.

TABLE 4:
COMMON FORMS OF RESISTANCE

Form of Resistance	Often Said	Explanation
Denial	"There's no problem here"	Denial of the problem or the credibility of the case for change. Often blame the victims.
Refusal (of responsibility)	"It's not my job to do something about it."	Refusal to recognize responsibility.
Inaction	"It's not a priority right now"	Refusal to implement a change initiative.
Placate	"Yes, yes. We must do something...one day."	Efforts to appease or pacify those advocating for change in order to limit its impact.
Diminishing	"Of course we'd appoint more women, if only they were more experienced"	Simulating change while covertly undermining it.
Shifter	"What about men's rights" Men are victims too, you know"	Shifting progressive frameworks and goals to meet another groups agenda
Reversal	"We tried that once and women didn't want to take up the promotion/training opportunity"	Reversing or dismantling a change initiative.
Extreme	"These feminists deserve to have push back, don't they see it's been like this forever?"	Aggressive, attacking response.
Separateness	"I don't want to be involved in this because my credibility will be questioned"	Women that want to separate from GD&I to protect themselves from missing out on future opportunities.
Competitive	"There are only so few positions at the top and if anyone is going to fill that senior job, it's me!"	Women sharpening their elbows and competing for positions and not supporting one another.

▷ Guidelines for Managing Resistance

To have the least amount of resistance, you need to have a systematic process in place, starting with clear messaging from the top with an accompanying communications plan, a leader/sponsor actions map, and individual coaching and training. For more details on developing a resistance strategy, go to www.centreforsocialintelligence.ca. I have developed a plan to eliminate resistance that is comprised of three interdependent strategies for leadership, communications, and HR that when implemented, effectively reduces resistance.

Establishing general guidelines for managing resistance *before* it is encountered during the project will increase the effectiveness of the overall implementation of the strategy. An effective process for creating a resistance strategy includes:

1. Identifying the root cause of resistance (through employee feedback, supervisor input, compliance audits)
2. Addressing the root cause of this resistance through personal coaching (See the top ten list in the following pages.)
3. Providing ongoing coaching opportunities and gathering feedback from the employee or manager over a defined period of time
4. Communicating the consequences of not supporting gender diversity and inclusion
5. Implementing the consequences of not supporting gender diversity and inclusion

Part of building awareness around the need for the GDI strategy is ensuring that business leaders have created a compelling reason for *why the strategy is needed and what the risk of not implementing it is*. Your compelling case for change reduces the level of resistance right from the onset; however, it doesn't work for everyone.

Meeting such resistance can be frustrating. Yet the majority of it can be overcome if managed correctly. Some of the most successful tactics for managing resistance are:

- Listening and understanding objections: Being heard is critical. Listening can also provide managers with an opportunity to clear up misunderstandings by addressing rumors and misconceptions.
- Involving people and inviting ideas: Allowing employees to take ownership and insert their own ideas of supporting the change.
- Convert the strongest dissenters: Through one-on-one discussions, focus on the individual(s) that are the most vocal in their dissent and turn them around. If you can show them why an increase in gender diversity and inclusion is needed, these individuals will become allies and likely become equally vocal in their support of the initiative.

It's important to note that middle managers have the highest level of influence with their peers and teams. Leaders in the middle vary in disposition and range from strong leaders who build a trusting environment to supervisors who are feared by their employees. They play a significant role in the adoption of the GDI strategy. During the change, these managers have the power to either help or hinder the GDI task force's work. They may be a(n):

- **Advocate** who acts in favour of the change and helps with implementation.
- **Neutralizer** who revises messages from executive sponsors and the GDI task force and tailors it to meet their own agenda.
- **Renegade** who's unpredictable, sometimes appearing to support the change and other times undermining the change at vital points in the process.
- **Villain** who deliberately and proactively sabotages the GDI strategy using their own position of power and authority and their informal communication network with peers and executives.

For different levels within an organization, there are also tactics that have proven successful, such as:

- **Executives:** building an emotional connection to how morally just it is to provide meaningful opportunities to women and building a logical connection to the benefits, both financially and culturally, of doing so.
- **Mid-level Managers:** helping team members integrate their responsibility to drive a gender-inclusive culture with their existing job requirements, supporting them along the way, and reassuring them that the end result will be a more effective workplace.
- **Employees:** Clearly describing expectations for behaviour in a modern workplace that is inclusive of women and other cultures, understanding and addressing their concerns, providing training and coaching, and reassuring them that new policies and programs will benefit the entire workforce.

The following is a list of the top ten strategies for managing resistance when implementing a GDI strategy. Details for each strategy follow the initial list.

Top Ten Actions for Managing Resistance

1. Listen and Understand Objections.
2. Focus on the "What" and Let Go of the "How."
3. Remove Barriers.
4. Provide Simple, Clear Choices and Consequences.
5. Create Hope.
6. Show the Benefits in a Real and Tangible Way.
7. Make a Personal Appeal.
8. Convert the Strongest Dissenters.
9. Create a Financial Incentive and/or Give Recognition.
10. Create an Example.

1. Listen and Understand Objections.

A critical step any manager should take to create a desire to implement a GDI strategy is to listen. The power of true listening and *empathy* is often underestimated. In many cases, employees simply want to voice their objections and be heard. Understanding these objections will provide a clear path toward resolution.

Listening to objections also helps managers identify misunderstandings about the focus on gender diversity and inclusion. Rumours and background conversations often produce incorrect messages and wrong perceptions. Only through listening will managers identify these misperceptions and provide a correct and clear story about what is taking place.

When listening to employees' objections, managers must avoid debating or arguing with employees. The goal is to listen, understand, and provide clarity about the process and end goal toward gender equality in the organization.

2. Focus on the "What" and Let Go of the "How."

In some instances, it is effective for managers to let go of the "how" and simply communicate "what" needs to change. Transfer ownership of the solution to employees.

Communicate a clear vision of the end state, along with specific goals and timelines with employees. Employees then take on actually achieving that vision. Employee involvement and ownership naturally builds desire to support the GDI culture shift and ensures that employee objections are addressed in the solution.

This technique sometimes requires greater resources to engage people in information-gathering sessions, but uniting many teams at the same time creates a "full-court press" and builds momentum on the issue across the organization.

3. Remove Barriers.

When listening to and understanding objections, personal beliefs and biases may be revealed that prevent an individual from accepting gender equality.

Coaching, education, and training helps individuals air their views and learn new responses to what is happening. Though very often these interventions bring folks around, sometimes you have a "Hugh" dissenter. In that case, additional actions are required.

4. Provide Simple, Clear Choices and Consequences.

Ultimately, it's up to each and every employee to make a choice to practice gender diversity and inclusion in the workplace. Managers facilitate the GDI strategy by being clear about the choices available to employees in an effort to support staff. For example, managers can offer the choices of:

- Speaking directly with the manager about why they're in resistance
- Speaking with a coach
- Attending training
- Becoming the business unit representative on the project team, which will allow them to learn and see firsthand why the change is important to the organization

In the absence of pursuing one of the suggested actions, it's important leaders articulate the consequences of inaction, which may not be too favourable. If the culture of the company is moving in a direction that an individual can't or won't accept, it may be time for the individual to find work with a more palatable culture.

5. Create Hope.

Many people respond positively to the opportunity for a better future. They want to have hope.

Senior leaders and middle managers may create conditions for successful adoption by sharing their own passion for it, creating excitement, enthusiasm, and hope in a better future for employees and the organization. People like to follow a leader who creates hope and whom they respect and trust. Having senior leadership exhibit regular, visible, and active participation in the GDI strategy creates hope and energy around the future state of gender equality and inclusion.

6. Show the Benefits in a Real and Tangible Way.

For some employees, seeing is believing. Demonstrating the benefits of a GDI strategy in a real and tangible way spurs on employees. Some ideas for doing this include:

- Sharing stories about other companies who have successfully implemented a GDI strategy
- Inviting guests to provide personal testimonials outlining how they did it in their organization and how it benefited them
- Visibly demonstrating the success of pilot programs or trials within your own organization (Share small wins and celebrate success publicly.)

7. Make a Personal Appeal.

When a manager has a close working relationship with an employee, using a personal appeal to support the GDI strategy creates the motivation to be more accepting.

If the manager doesn't have a close relationship, they should look for an ally who can do this for them. A personal appeal works best with honest, open relationships where there is a high degree of trust and respect. A personal appeal may sound like:

- "I believe in this culture change."
- "This is important to me because . . ." (e.g., "I see my daughter entering this field one day," or "I've travelled to a lot of cultures and have respect for other ways of interacting with each other.")
- "I want your support."

In a personal appeal, there is both an emotional component and an expectations component. In other words, the leader says, "I'm counting on you." The emotional component is part of each person's desire to support the people they are close to and whom they trust.

The I'm-counting-on-you component implies that the employee is a valuable contributor to the organization's success. That kind of personal appeal and confidence in the individual's ability to get on board builds support for the GDI strategy.

8. Convert the Strongest Dissenters.

There is often a vocal dissenter you are working with who has made it known to you and others that they do *not* want to do anything differently. When you have one or more of these strong and vocal employees talking with anyone who will listen, they negatively influence many other employees within the organization.

Leaders should target these dissenters by using special tactics and interventions as outlined here to convert them to support the strategy. By doing so, the strongest dissenters sometimes become your strongest advocates. They become as vocal in their support as they were in their resistance.

Focus your energy on a few strong resistors rather than on large groups of employees, and two objectives are achieved for building positive momentum. First, you regain some control over the powerful background conversations that take place around the water cooler and during breaks. Second, you gain champions that are already influential among their peers.

9. Create a Financial Incentive and/or Give Recognition.

Another strategy for minimizing resistance is establishing a recognition program. Nothing makes people respond more quickly than the almighty dollar. Create financial incentives that tie GDI to the individual's performance measurement plan, define a goal that provides adequate representation of genders and reward employees when it is met, or use a peer recognition program to catch people "walking the talk" and reward them for it.

Another incentive is through awards and recognition. People like to be recognized for their efforts to align with what is being asked of them. Highlight their efforts in blog posts within the company, social media, or at corporate events. This will inspire others to follow suit.

I'm sure there are many financial incentives one could create to lead people toward the desired behaviour. Just implement what you can and watch how things change.

10. Create an Example.

Often a last resort, yet impactful example to others, is the removal of a key employee who is outwardly undermining GDI efforts. This sends a very clear signal that senior management takes this issue seriously and will not tolerate inequities of any kind. The message is:

- We are serious about this strategy moving forward.
- Resistance is futile and will not be tolerated.
- The consequences of not moving forward with the organizational goals are real and impactful.

This action basically boils down to a zero-tolerance policy. If you're at this stage with someone in your organization, this is their last opportunity to climb aboard the GDI train. If they don't, then chances are they are already looking for other employment.

Letting someone go doesn't need to be a negative experience for the employee. Termination packages containing severance pay, early retirement offerings, or a number of other programs could make it an agreeable process for the individual leaving and, at the same time, send the right message to the organization.

Note: This resistance management strategy should be considered only as a last resort. All other tactics should be explored prior to this one, as it can create a culture of fear and lead to unintended consequences. I believe that the majority of people who demonstrate resistance need a lot of coaching but eventually get there and do not need to be shown the door.

Case Study: Tolko Industries Ltd.

Tolko Industries Ltd. is a privately owned Canadian forest products company based in Vernon, British Columbia. Tolko's top executive is dedicated to creating a diverse, inclusive environment in the company and taking a leadership role to encourage diversity throughout Canada. In 2017, Tolko's CEO, Brad Thorlakson, demonstrated the company's commitment to leadership in gender diversity by signing the Minerva Foundation Pledge, created to generate a meaningful and sustainable increase in the representation of women leaders across all organizations and industries in British Columbia.[79]

Tolko Industries Ltd. was selected to become a member of the National Steering Committee for Gender Equity in Canada's Forest Sector—the first organization of its kind in Canada. Together with others in the forest sector, they are steering the development of a national action plan to increase gender diversity. Tolko offers a variety of training programs that give employees opportunities to learn how they can contribute to a diverse and inclusive workplace culture.

As an active and visible leader in gender diversity and inclusion, Tolko demonstrates its support through regular communications on actions undertaken with its employees and the sector. They've made GDI a part of their business strategy and are seeing results. It's their aim to create a workplace where all employees feel welcomed and valued as a member of the Tolko family.

▷ The Results

Tolko Industries' self-declaration option for all employees revealed that 16 percent of new hires in 2018 self-identified as First Nations, Métis, or Inuit. As a result, they saw the need and opportunity to introduce Indigenous Awareness Training for their leadership in Q1 2019. They also helped develop an Essential Skills Employment program for Indigenous peoples that was supported by two of their BC mills, resulting in several new hires. Finally, they enrolled in the Canadian Council for Aboriginal Business (CCAB) Progressive Aboriginal Relations certification program.

Regarding gender diversity, Tolko now employs roughly 14 percent women, up from 11 percent in 2016. Additionally, the number of females in the company has increased from 13.5 percent of total hires to almost 20 percent. The company has implemented actions and training to address identified development barriers. Recognizing that the company could do a better job supporting employees with growing families, they also updated Tolko's maternity and parental leave program.[80]

Takeaways

The statements below summarize the main points you can take away from this chapter.

- Appoint a gender diversity task force that includes representatives from different levels of the organization and different business units. The task force should work with the GDI officer to create a strategy.
- Create all components of a GDI strategy. They are all important.
- Do not react to resistance with surprise; expect it and plan for it. Be patient with individuals as they work their way through learning this new way of doing business.

Chapter 5:
LEVERAGE
THE CHANGE
INTO DOLLARS

To leverage the GDI actions undertaken in your organization, you must have gained wide acceptance that the workplace culture has evolved from your efforts, lending credibility to the idea that these changes will be sustained.

To *sustain* something means to keep it going in perpetuity. In our context, it means having gender diversity and inclusion integrated into corporate values and decision-making such that it is inherently woven into the corporate fabric of the workplace. In other words, a heightened awareness of gender and cultural differences is embedded so deeply into the culture that everyone is conscious of looking at things in the workplace through this lens.

Creating systemic changes—new practices, policies, and behaviours—is not a one-and-done effort. Strategies must evolve over time. they require continual evaluation and reinforcement to be considered effective. By measuring ongoing progress and responding with corrective actions to keep people *accountable*, results are manifested, including improvements to the bottom line.

With these results comes clarity on where to focus resources (human and financial) and what you can boast about to your employees and stakeholders. If you're wondering what you can highlight with your colleagues and peers, let me give you some ideas from a Harvard Business Review article[81] that states that a culture of diversity and inclusion leads to:

- Heightened morale among employees
- An evergreen learning culture
- Increases in innovation, productivity, and revenue
- An employer brand that becomes a magnet for top talent
- Increased retention of top talent
- A prosperous, democratic society

These are great highlights to share with internal and external communication channels to reach various audiences. I especially like the bonus of providing the foundation for a prosperous democracy—that's a huge benefit that isn't often mentioned. In the fast-changing interdependent, multicultural economy we live in, it's wonderful to think we can also contribute to the larger notion of democracy as a whole. So, overall, wouldn't those factors be great to claim as the reason you're doing this? And all of these benefits translate directly into dollars.

This chapter will outline the foundations of accountability for gender diversity and inclusion; including indicators to monitor and how to measure them, the benefits of recognition and creating a sense of belonging, and case studies to help spur your own thinking for what can be done in your own organization.

Accountability Is Key

According to Merriam–Webster, the word "accountable" is defined as "an obligation or willingness to accept responsibility or to account for one's actions." Straightforward enough. Synonyms include "responsible," "liable," "answerable," "reporting," and—I love this one—"obedient."

In terms of our current discussion, to be accountable means everyone playing a part in this, not just senior management. In an accountable culture everyone is responsible, liable, and answerable to their boss and colleagues in their words and actions. But, as we've already discussed, it starts with senior management saying and doing the right things, role-modelling, leading the way, and demonstrating that they can walk the talk while showing respect and empathy too. It also involves being accountable for providing recognition to those who are embodying the behaviours asked of them. But what is to be monitored, and how? Using a performance measurement strategy, you can identify what should be tracked and the means for doing so.

 Case Study: Lincoln Electric Holdings, Inc.

> **Lincoln Electric** Holdings, Inc. is an American multinational and a global manufacturer of welding products, arc welding equipment, welding consumables, plasma and oxy-fuel cutting equipment, and robotic welding systems. They employ 11,000 people around the world; their company officers and management committee is 27 percent gender diverse and inclusive. They claim a 30 percent diverse and inclusive board, and 60 percent of the engineers they recruited in 2018–19 are considered diverse.[82]
>
> The reason I highlight this company is because they recognize that this is a long-term strategy issue and that it matters to have diversity and inclusion in order to remain competitive. You have to embrace GDI as a *business strategy* and not do something piecemeal or half baked.
>
> "The reality is, the dynamics of the workforce continues to change. And for any business to be competitive, they need to attract the kind of talent they need for their long-term business strategy," said a top executive from

the company. The company also fosters dialogue by supporting employee programs, such as those for women in leadership and veterans, that allow teams to bounce ideas off one another and discuss how they fit in, their careers, or family life. Through their Diversity Council, senior management reports twice a year on GDI programs including talent attraction, retention, and succession planning. This keeps everyone *accountable* and allows employees to trust that management is taking GDI seriously.

Performance Measurement Strategy

A performance measurement strategy is a results-based management tool that is used to guide the selection, development and ongoing use of GDI performance measures. Its purpose is to assist the GDI Officer and task force to:

- Continuously monitor and assess the results of what is being monitored, as well as the approach chosen to monitor them
- Make informed decisions and take appropriate, timely action with respect to GDI actions undertaken
- Provide effective and relevant reporting on GDI actions
- Ensure that credible and reliable performance data are being collected to effectively support evaluation

It is important to remember that performance measurement and evaluation play complementary and mutually reinforcing roles. I define "evaluation" here to mean the systematic collection and analysis of evidence on the outcomes of programs to make judgments about their relevance and performance. Metrics help identify alternative, more efficient ways to deliver programs to achieve the same results.

Implementing effective performance measurement, in addition to supporting ongoing program monitoring, can also support and facilitate effective evaluation. Evaluation helps establish whether observed results are attributable (in whole or in part) to the GDI strategy and provide an in-depth understanding of why actions undertaken were or were not achieved.

What Should I Be Monitoring?

We all know the cliché: What gets measured gets done. Your organization's GDI strategy is no exception.

Making a concerted effort to track the progress toward gender equality and inclusion is needed if real change is to occur. Seeking parity between men and women has driven the development of metrics on a number of issues including the pay gap, the proportion of women in organizations, gender ratios across different levels, and career advancement opportunities, among others.

First, let's look at what should be tracked. Then we'll look at the various methods of tracking. From the research I've conducted, I see six key metrics that are useful for organizations to track and measure progress, including:

1. Pay
2. Recruitment
3. Retention
4. Advancement
5. Representation
6. Social Intelligence (Workplace Culture)

1. Pay

Achieving pay parity is something that should be straightforward to track and address. The global gender gap in economic participation stands at 58.5 percent, according to the World Economic Forum's Global Gender Report. Most of the countries in the aforementioned gender report have almost gotten rid of wage inequalities for the same work. For instance, in Britain, women make only 1 percent less than men who are at the same level and working in the same function, according to *The Economist*. However, the differential between the wages of men and women spike at the senior levels, where women have been found to make less than men. In Germany, Canada, and the United States, women at the senior level earn 15 to 20 percent less than men. To create equal pay opportunities, organizations need to first evaluate the existing wage gaps at different levels.

The next thing that should be closely scrutinized is the performance bonus and salary hikes. Assess whether men and women with same performance scores are being given (a) the same bonuses, (b) the same salary hikes, and (c) the same promotions. Once the (dis)parity is identified, organizations need to plan interventions.

A few suggestions on how to do this include:

- Have fixed pay ranges by position.
- Have fixed negotiation parameters.
- Calculate bonuses using hard metrics.

2. Recruitment

Biases in the hiring process exist before recruitment even begins. Recent research by Totaljobs found that the job descriptions of female-dominated roles used female-biased language, and vice versa for male-dominated roles.

The same bias transcends into the hiring process, as recruiters have often already made up their minds that they are going to hire a man (or a woman) for the job. Another study by Science for Work has found that men are preferred over females in male-dominated jobs such as consultants or management roles like CEOs. However, there is no disparity in selection for female-dominated jobs; a man is equally likely to be considered for a nursing role as a woman. While organizations have started to become more alert to gender bias while recruiting, there is still the threat of unconscious bias creeping in and corrupting decision-making.

To avoid any bias during recruitment, organizations need to keep an eye on the language used throughout the recruitment process. Determine whether job descriptions are gender-neutral and if the interviewers are being fair when asking questions.

The next thing that organizations need to do is track the entire recruiting funnel—the ratio of men and women applicants, the ratio of shortlisted candidates, the ratio of candidates called for the second interview, and so on. This can ensure that no strong female candidates miss out and give an overall picture of the trends regarding the ratio of men and women across the recruitment funnel. If the gap keeps increasing at every stage consistently for most of the roles, then there is a possibility that hiring managers are exhibiting unconscious bias.

Here are a few tips to help address this issue:

- **Blind screen candidates.** Keep gender out of resumes and consider blind interviews/assessments to reduce unconscious bias.
- **Outreach into key areas,** such as STEM opportunities. The hiring of women in STEM roles is still low, and it might require extra effort to reach out to more female candidates and entice them to apply.
- **Balance shortlisted men and women for job vacancies.** Try to create a fifty-fifty ratio of men and women candidates for job openings.
- **Diverse interview panels.** Have a representative panel of interviewers. A diversity of views reduces the chances for gender bias.

3. Retention

Companies also need to track women's attrition at different levels and the reasons behind it. Women are often equally represented at the entry-level positions, but the numbers dwindle as you move up the ladder. There seems to be a distinct shift in female representation when a woman starts a family. Offering parental leave for men helps balance this out because, if they are equally being offered leave to help raise the family, the conversation shifts at the workplace. It allows both men and women to contribute on the home front, creating greater social cohesion for all.

Companies should track the number of men and women at each level to identify where the career ladder is breaking. To retain women employees, organizations must ensure:

- **Flexible working policies:** For women employees who undergo maternity, the option of flexibility is a must.
- **Paternity leave:** This offers men the ability to help on the home front, demonstrating the importance of this role. It simultaneously shifts the workplace perspectives, levelling the playing field on opportunities for both women and men.
- **Male participation in diversity efforts:** It must not be an all-women affair. Anyone can occupy a leadership position, and that individual, regardless of gender, should be sensitive about diversity.

4. Advancement

According to McKinsey, the average wages of men are much higher than those of women. Women make 78 cents for every dollar made by men. This is due to the lack of women at senior high-paying roles. But if women aren't leaving the organization (as discussed above), then why are they not advancing to leadership positions? It is not for lack of career ambition.

This is another metric that organizations need to track very closely. Is it a case of women being discriminated against at the review stage? Is it a case of managers not trusting if women can devote adequate time to work? Is it a case of managers not considering women altogether for promotions? Or is there a skill gap that can be bridged? Organizations need to find the specific reasons behind the lack of advancement of women to senior positions and then address them with all stakeholders.

Possible interventions include:

- Sponsorship programs, where a senior executive champions a woman for advancement opportunities
- Professional development and executive coaching
- Visible diverse and inclusive role models, where women could seek them out and learn how they did it

5. Representation

Companies need to make sure women are represented across the executive level, and not just concentrated in female-dominated roles like HR. (Twenty-three percent of women in leadership positions are in HR.) This is another important metric that needs to be tracked.

Based on the growth patterns, women need to be encouraged to migrate to different functions, or even start their careers in traditionally male-dominated functions like strategy and sales. This can be addressed through:

- Technical training
- Stretch assignments in key areas
- Balanced shortlists of candidates

6. Social Intelligence in the Workplace Culture

Tracking social intelligence is an important aspect for companies to incorporate in their GDI metrics. Attaining respect for all employees, regardless of race or religion, requires skill development in the following areas:

- Greater *empathy* for different cultures and genders
- Greater *assertiveness* for women to find their voice, for men to speak up for women and themselves, and for all employees to be able to call out bad behaviour without fear of being ostracized

• Greater *impulse control* to prevent harassment from occurring in the first place

This list is not exhaustive, but it gives you a sense of the skills that, once developed, add new tools that increase the understanding and acceptance of gender diversity and inclusion in the workplace.

Potential platforms for increasing these skills are:

• Training and skills development
• Role-modeling
• Recognition for those performing the skills well

Measuring Performance

Many methods are available to track performance results, such as:

• Using surveys and assessments
• Monitoring engagement through informal feedback channels and networks
• Soliciting feedback by creating deliberate opportunities for dialogue
• Tracking usage or other implementation statistics for new programs and policies

A performance measurement strategy should ensure that SMART (specific, measurable, agreed-upon, realistic, and time-based) targets are in place. In other words, you are taking the things that need to be tracked, such as representation, and identifying what percentage you want to achieve in year one, year two, and so on until you get to your end goal.

You may have a GDI strategy that sets out to achieve full implementation within three years. Breaking it down by year and setting realistic targets helps create mindful change. Everyone in the company should be aware of the targets and should understand their role and responsibility in working toward that target.

Next, companies need to determine the methodology that will be used to monitor targets. How will progress be reviewed? How often? What measurement tools will be used? Below are some suggestions to consider for your own organization:

Quarterly Monitoring

- Conduct a gender audit of recruitment ratios for applicants, shortlists, and new hires.
- Collect gender ratios on promotions for positions with qualified male and female applicants.
- Analyze gender ratios of requests made and granted for flexible work arrangements.
- Research the percentage of women at each staff level and in each job description.

Yearly Monitoring

- Conduct an abridged gender audit annually that includes a selection of questions from the initial gender audit to measure lift.
- Hold a follow-up pay gap study using the same metrics as in the original study so that change can be evaluated.
- Review recruitment materials and targets and assess them for women's representation on recruitment shortlists.
- Track number, frequency, and attendance for gender-related training activities.
- Track reports of sexual harassment incidents.
- Review flexible work arrangements by gender.
- Review mentorship and professional development programs by gender.

Biennial Monitoring

- Repeat the full gender audit every other year.

Under the leadership of the GDI Officer, the task force should take charge of gathering all measurement results. After all of the necessary research has been collected, the task force should review and analyze data to identify ways to improve and sustain positive results. The task force might be able to conduct this task on its own, or they may decide to bring on a gender expert to assist.

Once the metrics have been collected and analyzed, it is time to review the process for accountability. Are the responsible team leaders aware of and trained in the progress they are striving to achieve? What specific accountability mechanisms are in place? For example, are results discussed during performance evaluations? Are results linked to bonuses?

The monitoring process should include a look at whether incentives are in place for teams and their managers that will serve to support continued investment in progress. The entire team should feel a sense of shared benefit and accomplishment.

A good analysis will identify patterns and themes and uncover those factors that led to success and those that limited effectiveness. Plan to address remaining gaps or new challenges that require attention to sustain the current path or advance in the next year's targets.

Sharing a clear summary of the findings in case studies with various audiences and through multiple communication methods will reinforce the momentum for change. Open a feedback loop that helps all employees communicate back about the overall effectiveness of the diversity and inclusion effort. It confirms to GDI Officers and other leaders that there is a continuing focus on achieving the intended business outcomes.

There are also other ways to effectively reinforce this GDI strategy within work units, the organization as a whole, and/or the industry overall:

- Provide workshops, training, and group activities to reinforce messages about gender diversity and inclusion.
- Continue to build the visibility of senior executives as champions for an inclusive workplace. Emphasize the need for

continued attention and commitment to the strategy for gender diversity and inclusion to sustain and continue to grow business success.

- Communicate status updates and gather and share success stories. For example, various groups may showcase to the rest of the company or the industry how they have shifted the work culture and successfully increased the participation of women and minorities in their work area.[83]

Tracking progress and celebrating successes will provide the foundation for leveraging your efforts into company recognition. By bringing internal successes to an external audience, the recognition shines a powerful light on the company culture, making it a magnet for top talent. With that top talent, you kick-start the value proposition identified in chapter 1. You will have successfully leveraged your efforts and created a return on your investment in your GDI strategy.

 ## Case Study: Johnson & Johnson (Part 1)

As of 2020, Johnson & Johnson employs 130,000 people around the world, has given 51 percent of global promotions to women in the last year, and has spent $1.42 billion USD with diverse suppliers in the last year. Recognizing that you can impact the supply chain on this topic is something people don't usually think about, but it makes a huge impact. Write procurement policies that ensure a certain amount of the supply chain is diverse and inclusive.

Johnson & Johnson recognizes that its target market is comprised of diverse and inclusive consumers, and, as such, it behooves them to have their internal teams represent this diversity, too. Their approach creates innovative solutions to their product development and maximizes their marketing efforts. More specifically, Johnson & Johnson:

- Makes multicultural marketing a foundational competency by training their marketers to integrate it into their business plans
- Leverages their Employee Resource Groups (ERGs) to provide ongoing input to their multicultural marketing strategy, as well as creative and innovative feedback to brands. For example, their GenerationNOW's millennial moms shared insights on advertising concepts for their Johnson's Baby products relaunch, resulting in ads with higher quantitative testing scores.
- Is a founding member of the Unstereotype Alliance. Convened by UN Women, the Unstereotype Alliance tackles the widespread prevalence of gender bias that is often perpetuated through advertising.
- Has delivered on their Health for Humanity 2020 goal focused on supplier diversity. As reported in their 2018 Health for Humanity Report, Johnson & Johnson consistently achieves benchmark spending with U.S. diverse and small suppliers and is working to double the number of countries with established supplier D&I programs.

Additional measures of accountability involve an Inclusion Index that is part of their bi-annual employee engagement survey, which is called the Our Voice Survey. In 2017, the company's Our Voice Survey, with a participation rate of 87 percent, showed that an overwhelming majority of employees believed that Johnson & Johnson was a place where diverse perspectives were valued, and almost all employees believed that their supervisors treated them with respect. These results speak volumes about the company culture, and, while there is always more to be done, it's a good indication that they're on the right track.

Johnson & Johnson supports their leaders who want to improve the inclusiveness of their teams through tools and resources, including their internal GDI networks. They maintain systems of accountability through a variety of programs, behavioural expectations and controls, and their performance management policies.

Sustaining Behaviour Changes

Many training offerings are necessary on the journey toward a more diverse and inclusive culture. Topics include learning what diversity even means, unconscious bias training, skills development on social intelligence, and beyond. Programs create sponsoring and mentoring opportunities and establish GDI networks. These connections create a forum for diverse views to be brought to light and establish common ground.

GDI training and programs need to be monitored and must be evergreen to evolve with updated priorities. According to International Finance Corporation Insights, companies can monitor their efforts in three ways:[84]

Corporate-wide monitoring[1]: Qualitative and quantitative monitoring should take place throughout the duration of training. Training deliverables should be integrated into corporate key performance indicators (KPIs). This will require new KPIs to be established. By integrating these

---

[1] Reprinted with permission

training deliverables into formal performance indicators, the monitoring process is simplified. Such monitoring systems make it easier to measure progress on diversity and inclusion goals (for example, the number of females promoted to senior leadership within the year).

Informal, case-by-case monitoring of participant development: Managers/supervisors of training participants should provide qualitative feedback on development, both formally and informally. At a minimum, managers should provide feedback on retention and application of training deliverables as they conduct performance reviews. This feedback will support the data captured by the human resources department. In addition, it holds managers more accountable for ensuring learning retention of new behaviours and their application.

Program monitoring: Continuous monitoring of the training programs themselves is important. This ensures that the training offered continues to meet the needs of participants—needs that can change over time. Comprehensive program feedback forms and the monitoring of delivery systems can enable better control over content. This helps identify the kinds of changes necessary to ensure the continued relevance of learning modules. A GDI expert can be brought in on a biannual basis to check on training to be sure that materials are current.

Maintaining, internalizing, and building on skills learned is an essential investment in training. The easiest way to ensure the sustainability of skills is to create multiple and mutually reinforcing touchpoints.

• Managers/supervisors: They must play a central role in reinforcing new learning. This means having an

understanding of program content so they can support participants as learned skills are applied. Social intelligence training will help the manager discover what skills are needed with his/her team.

- *Reinforcement systems: Formal mentorship/sponsorship programs help reinforce the learning and contribute to sustaining gains. They give participants the opportunity to test out and review the skills learned. Such programs also provide valuable exposure to senior decision-makers who could advocate on behalf of their mentees in the future.*

- *Continuing networking opportunities at local, regional, and global levels: This allows ongoing interaction among participants long after the training has ended. Such opportunities are particularly important for the development of both hard and soft skills, because they enable the sharing of best practices, lessons learned, and feedback. Summits for high-potential leaders provide similar opportunities to continue conversations around learning while acknowledging the accomplishments of successful women and men.*

Recognition and a Sense of Belonging

Recognizing individual employee and team achievements improves morale and brings additional benefits beyond that. Award programs and other incentives contribute to a company's internal and external branding and become a beacon for others to know that if they work there, there is a high likelihood of a supportive workplace culture.

Companies that maintain a dynamic and prosperous workplace for all are able to attract the best talent. They also create better well-being and a healthier workplace culture, which means less turnover and fewer sick days. Suddenly the GDI strategy converts a positive corporate culture into real dollars.

Companies that embrace a GDI strategy are well-positioned to earn national and global recognition for Best Workplace Culture or other human resource awards. Current recognition lists are the "100 Best Companies for Women" and the "DiversityInc. Top 50." Getting certified as a gender-diverse workplace can also help raise a company's profile.

I mentioned them earlier in the book, but let me expand the point. There is a workplace gender equality certification organization called EDGE, or Economic Dividends for Gender Equality. They have defined bronze, silver, and gold standards; and once a company is audited, EDGE will provide recognition for companies that meet their criteria.

The notion of an international certification led me to think it would be even more effective if we did something nationally and created gender equality certification right at the sector level. For example, there are currently certification bodies in the forest sector that focus on the environmental aspects of a company to ensure that it is managing their forests in a sustainable manner. I propose that we create something similar for gender equality, embedding the social aspect into the already-built sectoral certification bodies. That way companies will aspire to be recognized for achieving sustainable development. They will do all they can environmentally and socially to ensure that their business is operating at the best of its ability and not incurring a financial loss as a result of these efforts.

The importance of recognizing companies that are fulfilling gender diversity and inclusion expectations and adhering to indicators cannot be overstated. A study conducted by Culture Amp and Paradigm, surveying 7,000 individuals from 35 organizations, found that having a sense of belonging was the metric most tied to workplace commitment and motivation, especially for underrepresented groups.[85]

To ensure that more people are recognized, the parties responsible for giving recognition must themselves be diverse. If executives are giving recognition, their limited perspectives will be the only determinant for what is celebrated and rewarded. If companies empower everyone to recognize and reward each other, the scope of who and what is recognized will result in more employees experiencing a sense of belonging.

To increase the impact of recognition, it should be visible to everyone in the company and its stakeholders.[86] One way to achieve this level of transparency is to initiate gender diversity awards programs. Not only do awards programs reinforce positive behaviour, but they also help position the company as an employer of choice for future employees.

Here are just a few examples of awards programs to aspire to. There are many now popping up by sector. Seek out what is happening in your network to find one that is most relevant for your business.

> **WEP CEO Leadership Awards**: The awards program of the Women's Empowerment Principles initiative recognizes concrete and innovative actions by CEOs to advance the Women's Empowerment Principles.
>
> **Catalyst Awards**: These awards recognize efforts to support the recruitment, development, and advancement of all women, including diverse women. Qualifications for the award include a thorough examination of candidates' initiatives; including an onsite evaluation to evaluate proven, measurable results that benefit women across a range of dimensions, such as race/ethnicity, sexual orientation, gender identity, religion, generation, nationality, disability, and indigenous or aboriginal peoples.

DiversityInc.: The DiversityInc. Hall of Fame is for companies taking exemplary actions to incorporate diversity and inclusion in the workplace.[87] Two case studies included in this book represent companies that have made the list, Johnson & Johnson and Sodexo. The criteria for the Hall of Fame are a helpful guide on what to pursue:

- *Human Capital Diversity Metrics*: a gender and racial/ethnicity breakdown of representation in overall workforce representation, overall management, senior management, new hires, promotions, and the 10 percent highest-paid populations

- *Leadership Accountability*: CEO/senior leadership commitment and accountability, board of directors, office of diversity and inclusion, and diversity council practices and representation metrics

- *Talent Programs*: employee resource groups, mentoring, high potential and sponsorship programs, practices, and participation metrics

- *Workplace Practices*: talent acquisition, talent management, onboarding, diversity training, workforce development and engagement, LGBT, people with disabilities, military community, and employee benefits policies and practices

- *Supplier Diversity*: procurement with companies owned by people from underrepresented groups, accountability, and practices

- *Philanthropy*: contributions to non-profit organizations focused on people from underrepresented groups, employee volunteerism, and matching programs and practices

Case Study: Johnson & Johnson (Part 2)

In 2018, Johnson & Johnson continued to lay the foundation for their leaders and employees to be inclusive in everything they do. Achievements include having implemented awards and recognition programs such as the following:

- A global Diversity & Inclusion Honors program to celebrate best-in-class approaches that drive business impact across their three strategic pillars
- The #BelongatJNJ campaign for employees to share their personal GDI stories
- TEDxJNJ events hosted by their Office of Creative Engagement to enable employees to share their unique stories and experiences.[88]

 Case Study: L'Oréal

L'Oréal USA has certainly done its part toward GDI with the launch of Think Tanks, employee resource groups that promote a more inclusive workplace for underrepresented groups, including women, people of colour, people with disabilities, veterans, and the LGBTQ community. Think Tanks have helped L'Oréal USA identify policies and programs to better support their diverse workforce, including offering new disability benefits and health-care coverage for infertility treatment and gender reassignment surgery. L'Oréal USA's Think Tank members are also providing valuable marketing insights to help the company authentically build a dialogue with diverse audiences across its brands.

Different Think Tanks have different missions. For instance, the "L'Oréal for Women" Think Tank developed a road map to support the advancement of women into senior positions. Two key initiatives were a leadership certification program at Harvard Kennedy School and an annual offsite for senior leaders that focused on promoting equality and fighting bias. Since the program started in 2012, L'Oréal USA has seen a 40 percent increase in women in leadership positions and an 18 percent increase in people of color across the company. During the same time period, the number of employees who have disclosed a disability has quadrupled.[89]

This evolution is due in part to the commitment to equity from our top leadership, as well as ongoing actions taken by teams at both a local and global level. In 2019, L'Oréal Group was ranked as one of the most gender-balanced companies worldwide by Equipleap. L'Oréal has worked with INED (the French Institute for Demographic Studies) since 2007 to analyze the gender pay gap in France. Since 2017, the group has deployed this methodology internationally. L'Oréal is also regularly audited to obtain the Gender Equality European and International Standard in twenty-three countries and EDGE (Economic Dividends for Gender Equality) certifications in seven countries. In 2018, L'Oréal was one of the most committed companies in the creation of the "One in Three Women" Program against gender-based domestic violence.

Return on Investment: The ROI on GDI

Having walked through developing a GDI strategy, you can see now that it follows a logical path on implementation. But I'm sure you're asking, "But where do I see the ROI?" Let me take you back to the value proposition.

It's the creation of a workplace culture that creates the magnet for top talent. As we've discussed, there are various tools and strategies to achieve that, and they all lead to the end goal of a respectful workplace culture that drives performance and innovation.

Remember the Sodexo example I gave early on? They invested in rolling out a GDI strategy and now claim a $19 ROI for every dollar spent. This is an impressive example of the higher performance a company achieves with this work. But let's get humble for a moment and, say, your ROI is only half that. Is it still worth the effort for a $9-10 ROI for every dollar you spend? From my experience, we are quite satisfied with returns like that from the stock market, so how can you go wrong?

The Value of Taking Action

Some quick reminders on the value of taking action. According to Deloitte Insights, organizations with a diverse and inclusive culture are:

- 2x as likely to meet or exceed financial targets
- 3x as likely to be high-performing
- 6x more likely to be innovative and agile
- 8x more likely to achieve better business outcomes[90]

According to Cisco, a company that has proven results on GDI performance, measuring the return on investment for GDI data indicates that a company's efforts impact many key business indicators or metrics, such as:

- Positive vs. negative public relations

- Customer surveys and loyalty
- Productivity
- Market penetration
- Profitability
- Employee satisfaction surveys, evaluations, and retention
- Number of discrimination complaints
- Equal employment opportunity and affirmative action metrics
- Number of underrepresented employees in employee resource groups
- Number of underrepresented employees promoted in senior leadership and on boards of directors
- Percentage of diversity objectives aligned the company's key strategic objectives
- Accountability and incentive assessments

Your people are your greatest asset. Investing in them will create the social return on investment that you're looking for.

Takeaways

The statements below summarize the main points you can take away from this chapter.

- Create a GDI performance measurement strategy that tracks indicators and holds everyone accountable.
- Demonstrate support and commitment to GDI by affiliating with global, national, and/or sector-wide recognition programs.
- Recognize employees' efforts to promote GDI through internal recognition and awards. This will create a strong sense of belonging and a beacon for top talent.
- By doing this, it will show you how you have leveraged your change efforts into dollars.

Conclusion

Rita Sola Cook, the Midwest region executive for Global Commercial Banking at Bank of America Merrill Lynch, said it best when she said, "The passion is palpable when you feel the company you work for is doing the right thing." And I argue that gender diversity and inclusion is squarely one of those right things, for women, men, business, and society.

McKinsey studied seventeen leading companies engaging successfully in diversity and inclusion and affirmed what this book proposes. "More diverse companies are better able to attract top talent, to improve their customer orientation, employee satisfaction, and decision-making."

The study found that, although progress "has been slow on average, individual companies have made real strides in improving their GDI outcomes and in effectively using these results to influence business outcomes."

The study identified four key components of achieving success through GDI:

1. Commit and Cascade
2. Link GDI to Growth
3. Create an Initiative Portfolio
4. Customize for the Desired Impact.[91]

In practical terms, leaders must commit to a vision and hold middle management accountable for the results. Your business growth strategy must also be linked to your GDI initiatives in an explicit manner and backed up by hard data. As such, your portfolio of GDI initiatives needs to be targeted based on growth priorities and customized based on your industry or geographic region, etc., to ensure buy-in and maximize impact not just within your organization but across your business sector as a whole.

This study, as well as what has been shared in the first chapter regarding the value proposition, makes a strong case for how companies are using diversity and inclusion as a business advantage. When senior executives make this commitment, the resulting improvements in areas such as turnover and retention, company morale, stakeholder support, and financial performance cannot be denied.

The Five-Step GDI Blueprint

Throughout this book, we have outlined what effective GDI looks like, why it is important, and how to integrate it into your organization. These key takeaways can form the blueprint for your GDI strategy and position your company to be more diverse and stronger than ever.

1. Identify the Value Proposition

- The cost-benefit analysis of implementing a gender diversity and inclusion strategy shows greater returns than if nothing was in place.
- The potential liability of an employee or peer who decides to go rogue and engage in inappropriate behaviour in the workplace can be extremely costly.
- The economic benefits will push you, and the legislation will pull you toward action on gender diversity and inclusion.
- Turnover of employees will decrease—for women *and* for men.

- There will be:
  - ◇ Increased profitability and productivity
  - ◇ Enhanced ability to attract and retain talent
  - ◇ Greater creativity, innovation, and openness
  - ◇ Enhanced company reputation
  - ◇ Better ability to gauge consumer interest demand

2. Utilize Corporate Social Intelligence

- Diversity and inclusion is an everybody issue, not just a women's issue.
- Social intelligence is comprised of a suite of skills that should be made part of the values in any company to have a culture that is accepting of diversity and inclusion.
- By onboarding social intelligence, companies can see greater support for gender diversity and inclusion, leading to greater performance, innovation, and creativity, and better business outcomes.

3. Be the Change

- Participate in events that allow leaders across your sector to share knowledge and discuss progress on gender advancement within their companies.
- There are many actions you can take right away to get things started. If you don't know what to do, take time with a gender expert coach to position yourself to move forward.
- Be visible and take action often. Be a challenger within your executive team when it comes to their words and actions.
- Stay engaged.

4. Make the Change

- Appoint a gender diversity task force that includes representatives from different levels of the organization and different

business units. The task force should work with the GDI Officer to create a strategy.
- Create all components of a GDI strategy—they are all important!
- Do not react to resistance with surprise—expect it and plan for it. Be patient with individuals as they work their way through learning this new way of doing business.

5. Leverage the Change

- Create a GDI performance measurement strategy that tracks indicators and holds everyone accountable.
- Demonstrate support and commitment to GDI by affiliating with global, national, and/or sectoral recognition programs. Recognize employees' efforts to promote GDI through internal recognition and awards. This will create a strong sense of belonging and a beacon for top talent.
- By doing this, it will show you how you have leveraged your change efforts into dollars.

As we have seen, *not* taking action to increase diversity and inclusion—in large and small organizations alike—becomes a poor business decision. And as content like this book reaches a wider audience, showing the value and the way of GDI, successful leaders will seize the opportunity to *lead the change.* It's up to you to be one of them.

Centre for Social Intelligence

Depending on where you are in your organization's journey toward GDI, all this may seem daunting. Fortunately, you don't have to do it alone.

Whether it's through sector-wide national action plan that affects change on gender diversity and inclusion or it's a company-wide effort, the Centre for Social Intelligence (CSI) knows how to work strategically with leaders to make real change. We coach leaders on how to plan, design, and implement company-wide strategies with the least amount of resistance from employees. Working in your specific context, we also guide leaders on their role as the sponsors of the strategy, including new language and skills to ease the conversation with the most reluctant middle managers.

Measuring and tracking progress, getting recognition either through sector awards, HR awards or certifications such as EDGE certification, leaders will see results and attract the best and brightest, spurring innovation and better performance. And they focus beyond gender to include those with disabilities too.

How CSI Can Help

CSI was created to address the economic benefits of social dimensions in the workplace. When CSI was founded in 2013, social issues like gender equality were not yet seen as a means of creating greater organizational performance. CSI responded to this gap and has worked effectively with public, private, and not-for-profit groups to empower them to create change in their organizations. We specialize in coaching leaders and providing the necessary tools and skills to develop themselves and their teams in a way that results in a respectful, sustainable, and profitable work environment for all.

CSI Associates; which include experts in the area of gender equity, change management, and gender auditing and research; are able to guide organizations through questions like "Where do I start?" and "How do I get there?" We work with you to identify your goals and empower you to achieve them.

Interested in making a big impact in your sector? Based on experience in the natural resource sectors, CSI will help you create a national gender equity sector action plan, engaging all stakeholders, including public, private, not-for-profit, academia, and Indigenous representatives from across your sector. Through this national sector approach, CSI will create a sustainable workplace culture change, improving the image of the sector overall.

Based on the current status of actions undertaken to date, CSI will help your organization to develop a gender strategy to bring you from simply complying with employment equity/human rights legislation to being a gender champion that others aspire to work with and for. There are many different gender equity tools to choose from, and CSI can work with you to determine which ones are best suited to your needs.

Using internationally recognized indicators, CSI will conduct a gender audit in your organization to show where there are gaps in your policies, procedures, and culture that, once addressed, will create a more welcoming workplace for everyone. Establishing baseline information and strategically deciding where to invest your time and resources is a solid first step to moving your business forward.

The gender gap audit assessment will look at:

- Gender-based pay gaps
- Recruitment and promotion
- Leadership development training and monitoring
- Family-work balance
- Corporate social intelligence
- Public image

You know that your organization could do better and become a more gender-balanced workforce, but how do you present a case to your C-suite that will make them pay attention? Visit the CSI website at www.centreforsocialintelligence.ca/associates/and download a free guide that explains how and what to include in your business case. We cover topics that your executive and stakeholders care about, like profitability, performance, sustainability, and more.

If you want to take your level of commitment one step further, contact me at 613-252-9694, and let's get started. Let us help you lead the change.

Acknowledgements

To my husband Mark for his endless belief in me.

To Lauren and Luke. I hope your life experiences transcend the gender inequality I have experienced and that you take care to respect diversity for everyone, no matter what the race or religion, as that will be more the norm in your lifetime than it has been in mine.

And finally, to all senior decision-makers. I hope you use this book to spark conversation and action in your spheres of influence.

About the Author

Kelly Cooper, B.Sc., M.A. is the Founder and President of the Centre for Social Intelligence (CSI). Ms. Cooper helps leaders transform their organizations to be more gender diverse and inclusive through coaching, communications, training, and skills development. Her company also conducts gender gap audit assessments, develops GDI strat-  egies, and leads national sector-wide gender diversity action plans.

Ms. Cooper has been a guest speaker at various domestic and international conferences aimed at increasing women in senior executive roles and in technical positions. Her goal is to empower women *and* men with the necessary tools to create a respectful workplace where everyone contributes to higher performance and, ultimately, higher economic returns. At the core, GDI is not just a women's issue—it's an everybody issue. Multi-faceted actions are needed to effect sustained change. It starts with leadership.

Over her twenty-five-year career, Ms. Cooper has worked in Asia, Africa, Latin America, and Europe on various sustainable development projects. She holds a Master of Arts degree in International Environment, Development and Policy from the University of Sussex, UK, and an Honours Bachelor of Science degree from the University of Toronto, as well as certifications in GBA+, EQ-i 2.0, and ProSci change management (ADKAR model).

Endnotes

1 Coppin, Alan. *The Human Capital Imperative*. Palgrave Macmillan: Bourne End, Buckinghamshire, July 2017, 93–97. https://www.researchgate.net/publication/319173543_Diversity_and_Inclusion

2 "Definition of Gender Mainstreaming." International Labour Organization. https://www.ilo.org/public/english/bureau/gender/newsite2002/about/defin.htm

3 "Diversity Primer." Diversity Best Practices. Chapter 2: The ROI of Diversity and Inclusion, 25. https://www.diversitybestpractices.com/sites/diversitybestpractices.com/files/import/embedded/anchors/files/diversity_primer_chapter_02.pdf

4 An initial public offering (IPO) refers to the process of offering shares of a private corporation to the public in a new stock issuance. Public share issuance allows a company to raise capital from public investors.

5 McEnery, Thornton. "Goldman Sachs will no longer do IPOs for companies with all-male boards." *New York Post*, January 23, 2020. https://nypost.com/2020/01/23/goldman-sachs-will-no-longer-do-ipos-for-companies-with-all-male-boards/

6 "Women in Business Management: The business case for change." International Labour Organization, May 2019. 24. https://www.ilo.org/wcmsp5/groups/public/---dgreports/---dcomm/---publ/documents/publication/wcms_700953.pdf

7 "Women in Business Management: The business case for change," 25.

8 "The Windfall of Having More Women in Charge." Inc., March 23, 2015. https://www.inc.com/associated-press/for-business-more-women-in-charge-means-bigger-profits.html

9 Hunt, Vivian; Prince, Sara; Dixon-Fyle, Sundiatu; Yee, Lareina. "Delivering through Diversity." McKinsey & Company, January 2018, 14. https://www.mckinsey.com/~/media/McKinsey/Business percent20Functions/Organization/Our percent20Insights/Delivering percent20through percent20diversity/Delivering-through-diversity_full-report.ashx

10 Solomon, Charlene. "Unlocking the Business Benefits of Gender Diversity." CultureWizard. https://www.rw-3.com/blog/unlocking-the-business-benefits-of-gender-diversity

11 Solomon, "Unlocking the Business Benefits of Gender Diversity," June 29,2018. https://www.rw-3.com/blog/unlocking-the-business-benefits-of-gender-diversity

12 "Gender equality." Government.no, March 11, 2020. https://www.regjeringen.no/en/topics/equality-and-social-inclusion/likestilling-og-inkludering/gender-equality/id670481/

13 Lee, Linda-Eling. "The tipping point: Women on boards and financial performance." MSCI, December 13, 2016. https://www.msci.com/www/blog-posts/the-tipping-point-women-on/0538249725

14 Press release: "Diverse boards outperform male-only peers by US$655bn." GrantThornton, September 20, 2015. https://www.grantthornton.global/en/press/press-releases-2015/diverse-boards-in-india-uk-and-us-outperform-male-only-peers-by-us$655bn/

15 Noland, Marcus; Moran, Tyler; Kotschwar, Barbara. "Is Gender Diversity Profitable? Evidence from a Global Survey." Peterson Institute for International Economics, 2016, 8. https://www.piie.com/publications/wp/wp16-3.pdf

16 "Women in Business Management: The business case for change," 16.

17 Badal, Sangeeta. "The Business Benefits of Gender Diversity." Gallup, January 20, 2014. https://www.gallup.com/workplace/236543/business-benefits-gender-diversity.aspx

18 "Welcoming to Women: An Action Plan for Canada's Mining Employers." Women in Mining Canada, November 2016. https://wimcanada.org/wp-content/uploads/2017/01/WIM-NAP-book-full.pdf

19 "Gender Equality Benefits for Business Infographic." Global Compact Network Canada, September 28. https://www.globalcompact.ca/gender-equality-benefits-for-business-infographic/

20 "The Bottom Line: Connecting Corporate Performance and Gender Diversity." Catalyst Workplaces for Women, January 15, 2004. https://www.catalyst.org/research/the-bottom-line-connecting-corporate-performance-and-gender-diversity/

21 Baruah, 2018, https://www.academia.edu/39431981/Barriers_and_Opportunities_for_Women_s_Employment_in_Natural_Resource_Industries_in_Canada

22 Bourke, Juliet. *Which Two Heads are Better Than One? How Diverse Teams Create Breakthrough Ideas and Make Smarter Decisions.* Australian Institute of Company Directors, 2016.

23 Lagarde, Christine and Ostry, Jonathan D. "Economic Gains from Gender Inclusion: Even Greater than You Thought." IMFBlog, November 28, 2018. https://blogs.imf.org/2018/11/28/economic-gains-from-gender-inclusion-even-greater-than-you-thought/

24 Unlocking Opportunities for Women and Business: A Toolkit of Actions and Strategies for Oil, Gas, and Mining Companies." International Finance Corporation Insights, May 18, 2018.

25 Ibid.

26 "Gender Equality Benefits for Business Infographic." Global Compact Network Canada, September 28. https://www.globalcompact.ca/gender-equality-benefits-for-business-infographic/

27 Sunderland, Ruth. "After the crash, Iceland's women lead the rescue." *The Guardian*, February 21, 2009. https://www.theguardian.com/world/2009/feb/22/iceland-women

28 "Education in Canada: Attainment, Field of Study and Location of Study." Statistics Canada, July 25, 2018. https://www12.statcan.gc.ca/nhs-enm/2011/as-sa/99-012-x/99-012-x2011001-eng.cfm;

29 Ibid.

30 Stergiou-Kita, Mansfield, et al. "Danger Zone: Men, masculinity and occupational health and safety in high risk occupations." Canadian Institutes of Health Research, December 1, 2016. https://www.ncbi.nlm.nih.gov/pmc/articles/PMC4880472/

31 Ibid.

32 "Welcoming to Women: An Action Plan for Canada's Mining Employers." Women in Mining Canada, November 2016. https://wimcanada.org/wp-content/uploads/2017/01/WIM-NAP-book-full.pdf

33 "Welcoming to Women: An Action Plan for Canada's Mining Employers." Women in Mining Canada, November 2016. https://wimcanada.org/wp-content/uploads/2017/01/WIM-NAP-book-full.pdf

34 "Women in Business Management: The business case for change." International Labour Organization, May 2019. 24. https://www.ilo.org/wcmsp5/groups/public/---dgreports/---dcomm/---publ/documents/publication/wcms_700953.pdf

35 "The Future of Jobs." World Economic Forum, 2016. https://reports.weforum.org/future-of-jobs-2016/

36 Ibid.

37 "Women in Business Management: The business case for change," 24.

38 Glassdoor Team. "What Job Seekers Really Think About Your Diversity and Inclusion Stats." Glassdoor, November 17, 2014. https://www.glassdoor.com/employers/blog/diversity/

39 "Winning the fight for female talent: How to gain the diversity edge through inclusive recruitment." PwC, March 2017. https://www.pwc.com/gx/en/about/diversity/iwd/iwd-female-talent-report-web.pdf

40 Guardian staff and agencies. "Google paid former executives $35m after sexual assault allegation." *The Guardian*, March 11, 2019. https://www.theguardian.com/technology/2019/mar/11/google-executive-payout-harassment-amit-singhal

41 Gajanan, Mahita. "After CEO's Ouster, McDonald's Workers Sue Company Over 'Systemic Problem' of Sexual Harassment." *Time*, November 12, 2019. https://time.com/5725058/mcdonalds-sexual-harassment-lawsuit/

42 Campbell, Alexia Fernandez. "Why the gender discrimination lawsuit against Nike is so significant." *Vox*, August 15, 2018. https://www.vox.com/2018/8/15/17683484/ nike-women-gender-pay-discrimination-lawsuit

43 The Canadian Press. "Federal Court approves $900M deal to settle military sexual-assault cases." *The Sudbury Star*, November 26, 2019. https://www. thesudburystar.com/news/national/federal-court-approves-900m-deal-t o-settle-military-sexual-assault-cases

44 "Gender equality case nets nurses $150m." *CBC News*, July 3, 2012. https://www.cbc. ca/news/canada/ottawa/gender-equality-case-nets-nurses-150m-1.1257925

45 Mangione, Kendra and Molko, David. "RCMP agrees to cash settlements in sexual harassment, discrimination suit." CTV News, July 8, 2019. https://bc.ctvnews. ca/rcmp-agrees-to-cash-settlements-in-sexual-harassment-discriminatio n-suit-1.4498568

46 https://www.nytimes.com/2017/08/14/business/media/ fox-harassment-settlements-cost.html

47 The Canadian Press. "Motherhood, social norms behind gender wage gap in Canada: Finance Canada docs." *The Sudbury Star*, December 4, 2019. https://www. thesudburystar.com/news/national/motherhood-social-norms-behind-gender-wag e-gap-in-canada-finance-canada-docs

48 Sheth, Sonam; Gal, Shayanne; Hoff, Madison. "7 charts that show the glaring gap between men's and women's salaries in the US." *Business Insider*, March 31, 2020. https://www.businessinsider.com/ gender-wage-pay-gap-charts-2017-3#the-gender-wage-gap-varies-wid ely-depending-on-the-state-1

49 Woetzel, Jonathan; Madgavkar, Anu; Ellingrud, Kweilin; Labaye, Eric; Devillard, Sandrine; Kutcher, Eric; Manyika, James; Dobbs, Richard; Krishnan, Mekala. "How advancing women's equality can add $12 trillion to global growth." McKinsey Global Institute, McKinsey & Company, September 2015. https://www.mckinsey.com/ featured-insights/employment-and-growth/how-advancing-womens-equality-can-ad d-12-trillion-to-global-growth

50 "Government of Canada introduces historic proactive pay equity legislation." Government of Canada, October 29, 2018. https://www. canada.ca/en/employment-social-development/news/2018/10/ government-of-canada-introduces-historic-proactive-pay-equity-legislation.html

51 "Gender equality." Government.no, March 11, 2020. https://www.regjeringen. no/en/topics/equality-and-social-inclusion/likestilling-og-inkludering/ gender-equality/id670481/

52 Marinósdóttir, Mangea and Erlingsdóttir, Rosa. "This is why Iceland ranks first for gender equality." World Economic Forum, November 1, 2017. https://www.weforum.org/agenda/2017/11/why-iceland-ranks-first-gender-equality/

53 Chapman, Michael. "Gender Equality in Iceland." Guide to Iceland. https://guidetoiceland.is/history-culture/gender-equality-in-iceland

54 "Towards gender balanced parental leave." Australian Government Workplace Gender Equality Agency, October 11, 2017. https://www.wgea.gov.au/data/wgea-research/towards-gender-balanced-parental-leave

55 http://makeitourbusiness.ca/

56 "Welcoming to Women: An Action Plan for Canada's Mining Employers." Women in Mining Canada, November 2016. https://wimcanada.org/wp-content/uploads/2017/01/WIM-NAP-book-full.pdf

57 "Diversity Primer." Diversity Best Practices. Chapter 2: The ROI of Diversity and Inclusion. https://www.diversitybestpractices.com/sites/diversitybestpractices.com/files/import/embedded/anchors/files/diversity_primer_chapter_02.pdf

58 Gardenswartz et al. "Emotional Intelligence and Diversity: A Model for Differences in the Workplace", *Journal Of Psychological Issues in Organizational Culture*, Vol. 1, Number 1, 2010. 75. http://emotionalliteracyfoundation.org/research/Practitioners-corner-EIDI.pdf

59 Sherman, Kenneth C. *Journal Of Psychological Issues in Organizational Culture*, Vol. 1, 2016. https://onlinelibrary.wiley.com/journal/20418426

60 Steven Stein-Howard Book. *The EQ Edge: Emotional Intelligence and Your Success.* Jossey-Bass, 2011, 3rd Ed.

61 Kaufman, Michael. *The Time Has Come: Why Men Must Join the Gender Equality Revolution.* Counterpoint Press, 2019.

62 Ibid.

63 Drezner, Daniel W. "The tax on women in national security." *The Washington Post*, November 9, 2017. https://www.washingtonpost.com/news/posteverything/wp/2017/11/09/the-tax-on-women-in-national-security/

64 Shaw, Elyse; Hegemisch, Arinae; Hess, Cynthia. "Sexual Harassment and Assault at Work: Understanding the Costs." Institute for Women's Policy Research, October 15, 2018. https://iwpr.org/publications/sexual-harassment-work-cost/

65 Amaya, Laura; Schroder, Clare; Medrano, Sandra; Geertz, Alexandra. "Gender Equality is Not Just a Women's Issue." FSG, March 11, 2019. https://www.fsg.org/blog/gender-equality-not-just-women's-issue

66 "Women in the Workplace 2019." McKinsey & Company. https://womenintheworkplace.com

67 "Welcoming to Women: An Action Plan for Canada's Mining Employers." Women in Mining Canada, November 2016, 23–24. https://wimcanada.org/wp-content/uploads/2017/01/WIM-NAP-book-full.pdf

68 "40:40:20 For gender balance: Interrupting bias in your talent processes." Male Champions of Change, AAP Studio, 2019. https://malechampionsofchange.com/wp-content/uploads/2019/11/MCC-40-40-40-Talent-Processes-Toolkit-2019_Web_Final.pdf

69 Ibid. 23, 27, 31.

70 "Leadership Accord on Gender Diversity." Electricity Human Resources Canada. https://electricityhr.ca/workplace/diversity/accord/

71 "We Set the Tone: Eliminating Everyday Sexism," Male Champions of Change. 12. https://malechampionsofchange.com/wp-content/uploads/2018/04/We-Set-The-Tone_Eliminating-Everyday-Sexism.pdf

72 Unlocking Opportunities for Women and Business: A Toolkit of Actions and Strategies for Oil, Gas, and Mining Companies." International Finance Corporation Insights, May 18, 2018, 67.

73 "Welcoming to Women: An Action Plan for Canada's Mining Employers." Women in Mining Canada, November 2016. https://wimcanada.org/wp-content/uploads/2017/01/WIM-NAP-book-full.pdf

74 Ibid., 23.

75 Ibid.

76 https://www.centreforsocialintelligence.ca

77 Unlocking Opportunities for Women and Business: A Toolkit of Actions and Strategies for Oil, Gas, and Mining Companies." International Finance Corporation Insights, May 18, 2018.

78 "(En)countering resistance: Strategies to respond to resistance go gender equality initiatives." Victorian Health Promotion Foundation, 2018. 4.

79 "Diversity & Inclusion." Tolko. https://tolko.com/responsibility/diversity-inclusion/

80 Tolko. *Diversity & Inclusion Newsletter*, Summer 2019. 3. https://tolko.com/wp-content/uploads/2019/09/D_and_I_Newsletter_Summer_2019.pdf

81 Turban, Stephan; Wu, Dan; Zhang, Letian (LT). "Research: When Gender Diversity Makes Firms More Productive." *Harvard Business Review*, February 11, 2019. https://hbr.org/2019/02/research-when-gender-diversity-makes-firms-more-productive

82 "Diversity and Inclusion: Our Diversity Profile." Lincoln Electric. https://sustainability.lincolnelectric.com/diversity-inclusion.html#profile

83 "Welcoming to Women: An Action Plan for Canada's Mining Employers." Women in Mining Canada, November 2016. https://wimcanada.org/wp-content/uploads/2017/01/WIM-NAP-book-full.pdf

84 "Unlocking Opportunities for Women and Business: A Toolkit of Actions and Strategies for Oil, Gas, and Mining Companies." Tool Suite 1.15: Monitoring, Evaluation, and Reporting. International Finance Corporation Insights, May 18, 2018, 85–88.

85 Ciavolino, Emily. "Why Employee Recognition is Crucial to Inclusion." Bonusly, May 30, 2018. https://blog.bonus.ly/why-employee-recognition-is-crucial-to-inclusion

86 Ibid.

87 "DiversityInc Report Card." DiversityInc, 2019. https://www.diversityinc.com/media/2019/09/2019-DiversityInc-Report-Card_SAMPLE.pdf

88 "Diversity & Inclusion Impact Review." Johnson & Johnson.

89 "L'Oréal Ranked One of the Most Gender-Balanced Companies Worldwide by Equileap." L'Oréal, February 2, 2019. https://www.loreal.com/media/news/2019/october/equileap

90 Bourke. *Which Two Heads are Better Than One?*

91 Hunt, Vivian; Prince, Sara; Dixon-Fyle, Sundiatu; Yee, Lareina. "Delivering through Diversity." McKinsey & Company, January 2018. https://www.mckinsey.com/~/media/McKinsey/Business percent20Functions/Organization/Our percent20Insights/Delivering percent20through percent20diversity/Delivering-through-diversity_full-report.ashx

CPSIA information can be obtained
at www.ICGtesting.com
Printed in the USA
BVHW042149071122
651421BV00014B/130